CIMA

Certificate

BA4: Fundamentals of Ethics, Corporate Governance & Business Law

Course Book

For new syllabus assessments from January 2017

First edition August 2016

ISBN 9781509706341
ISBN (for internal use only) 9781509706389

eISBN 9781509707157

British Library Cataloguing-in-Publication Data
A catalogue record for this book is available from the
British Library

Published by

BPP Learning Media Ltd
BPP House, Aldine Place
142-144 Uxbridge Road
London W12 8AA

www.bpp.com/learningmedia

Printed in the United Kingdom by

Ashford Colour Press Ltd
Unit 600, Fareham Reach
Fareham Road, Gosport
Hampshire
PO13 0FW

Your learning materials, published by BPP Learning Media
Ltd, are printed on paper obtained from traceable
sustainable sources.

Contents

Welcome to BA4 Fundamentals of Ethics, Corporate Governance & Business Law

Description of the paper

The learning outcomes in this subject reflect the professional standards to be demonstrated for the benefit of all stakeholders. With this in mind, the place of ethics and ethical conflict is an essential underpinning for commercial activity. Ethics is more than just knowing the rules around confidentiality, integrity and objectivity. It's about identifying ethical dilemmas, understanding the implications and behaving appropriately. It includes the role of corporate governance, corporate social responsibility and audit; and their increasing impact in the management of organisations.

Wherever business is conducted the legal and administrative framework underpins commercial activity. With this in mind the areas of contact law, employment law, administration and management of companies is considered.

Syllabus Areas and their weighting

Weight

	Syllabus topic
30%	A. Business Ethics and Ethical Conflict
45%	B. Corporate Governance, Controls and Corporate Social
15%	C. General Principles of Legal System, Contract and Employment Law
10%	D. Company Administration

The Objective Test exam

Format	Computer Based Assessment
Duration	2 hours
Number of Questions	75 85
Marking	No partial marking – each question marked correct or incorrect All questions carry the same weighting (ie same marks)
Weighting	As per Syllabus Areas All component learning outcomes will be covered
Question Types	Multiple Choice Multiple Response Number Entry Drag and Drop Hot spot Item Sets
Booking availability	On demand
Results	Immediate

Verb Hierarchy

LEVEL 3

LEARNING OBJECTIVE

APPLICATION

How you are expected to apply your knowledge

VERBS USED	DEFINITION
Apply	Put to practical use
Calculate	Ascertain or reckon mathematically
Demonstrate	Exhibit by practical means
Prepare	Make or get ready for use
Reconcile	Make or prove consistent/compatible
Solve	Find an answer to/prove with certainty
Tabulate	Arrange in a table

LEVEL 2

LEARNING OBJECTIVE

COMPREHENSION

What you are expected to understand

VERBS USED	DEFINITION
Describe	Communicate the key features of
Distinguish	Highlight the differences between
Explain	Make clear or intelligible/state the meaning or purpose of
Identify	Recognise, establish or select after consideration
Illustrate	Use an example to describe or explain something

LEVEL 1

LEARNING OBJECTIVE

KNOWLEDGE

What you are expected to know

VERBS USED	DEFINITION
List	Make a list of
State	Express, fully or clearly, the details/facts of
Define	Give the exact meaning of

BPP
LEARNING MEDIA

5

Learning Outcomes

A. Business Ethics and Ethical Conflict (30%)

On completion of their studies, students should be able to:

Lead	Component	Level
1. Demonstrate an understanding of the importance of ethics to society, business and the professional accountant.	(a) Explain the nature of ethics and its application to society, business and the accountancy profession	2
	(b) Apply the values and attitudes that provide professional accountants with a commitment to act in the public interest and with social responsibility	3
	(c) Explain the need for a framework of laws, regulations and standards in business and their application and why CIMA and IFAC each have ethical codes	2
	(d) Distinguish between detailed rules-based and framework/principles approaches to ethics	2
	(e) Identify the ethical issues significant to organisations and how CIMA partners with strategic bodies to assist its members with ethical tensions/synergies	2
	(f) Describe how personal and organisational policies and values promote behaviour	2
2. Explain the need and requirements for CIMA students and members in adopting the highest standards of ethical behaviour.	(a) Explain the need to develop the virtues of reliability, responsibility, timeliness, courtesy and respect	2
	(b) Explain the fundamental ethical principles	2
	(c) Identify concepts of independence, scepticism, accountability and social responsibility	2
	(d) Illustrate the threats and safeguards to the fundamental ethical principles	2

Lead	Component	Level
3. Explain the various means of regulating ethical behaviour, recognising different parties' perspectives towards ethical dilemmas.	(a) Explain the relationship between the CIMA Code of Ethics and the law	2
	(b) Describe the consequences of ethical behaviour to society, business, the profession and the professional accountant	2
	(c) Identify conflicting perspectives of interest when dealing with stakeholders in society, business and values of professional accountants	2
4. Identify ethical dilemmas and how they may be resolved.	(a) Identify situations where ethical dilemmas and conflicts of interest occur, based on CIMA's ethical checklist	2

B. Corporate Governance, Controls and Corporate Social (45%)

On completion of their studies, students should be able to:

Lead	Component	Level
1. Explain the role of corporate governance in meeting the concerns of society and investors over the management of corporations.	(a) Describe corporate governance	2
	(b) Explain the interaction of corporate governance with business ethics and company law	2
	(c) Explain the interaction of corporate governance with business ethics and company law	2
	(d) Describe IFAC's main drivers of sustainable corporate success	2
	(e) Illustrate CIMA's practical proposals for better corporate governance	2
	(f) Distinguish between detailed rules-based and principles-based approaches to governance.	2

☆ OECD

Lead	Component	Level
2. Explain the impact of corporate governance on the directors and management structures of corporations.	(a) Describe the role of the board and different board structures	2
	(b) Explain the effects of corporate governance on directors' powers and duties	2
	(c) Describe the types of policies and procedures that constitute 'best practice'	2
	(d) Describe the respective committees and their roles and responsibilities with regards monitoring and controlling the actions of the Executive	2
3. Explain the role of external and internal audit.	(a) Identify the requirements for external audit and the basic processes undertaken	2
	(b) Explain the meaning of fair presentation	2
	(c) Distinguish between external and internal audit	2
	(d) Explain the purpose and basic procedures of internal audit; the need financial controls and the purpose of audit checks and audit trails	2
	(e) Explain the role of internal audit in non-financial monitoring and control activities	2
	(f) Illustrate the added value internal audit provides to both the board and management of the corporation	2
4. Explain the nature of errors and frauds.	(a) Explain the nature of errors	2
	(b) Explain the nature of fraud	2
	(c) Describe the different methods of fraud prevention and detection	2

Lead	Component	Level
5. Explain Corporate Social Responsibility (CSR) – a political and corporate perspective.	(a) Describe the OECD general policies	2
	(b) Explain the role of national and international laws and regulations	2
	(c) Describe conflicting demands of stakeholders	2
	(d) Identify issues with CSR and the supply chain	2
6. Explain the role of CSR within company reporting.	(a) Describe the guidelines of reporting CSR within annual reports	2
	(b) Identify synergies and tensions with CSR and brand management	2

C. General Principles of Legal System, Contract and Employment Law (15%)

On completion of their studies, students should be able to:

Lead	Component	Level
1. Explain how the law determines the point at which a contract is formed and the legal status of contractual terms.	(a) Identify the essential elements of a valid simple contract and situations where the law requires the contract to be in a particular form	2
	(b) Explain how the law determines whether negotiating parties have reached agreement and the role of consideration in making that agreement enforceable	2
	(c) Explain when the parties will be regarded as intending the agreement to be legally binding and how an agreement may be avoided because of misrepresentations	2
	(d) Explain how the terms of a contract are established and their status determined	2
	(e) Explain the ability of a company to contract	2

Lead	Component	Level
2. Explain the essential elements of an employment contract and best practice and the remedies available following termination of the contract.	(a) Explain how the contents of a contract of employment are established	2
	(b) Explain what work place policies and procedures are required either legally or recommended as best practice	2
	(c) Explain the distinction between unfair and wrongful dismissal and the consequences	2

D. Company Administration (10%)

On completion of their studies, students should be able to:

Lead	Component	Level
1. Explain the nature, legal status and administration of business organisations.	(a) Describe the essential characteristics of the different forms of business organisations and the implications of corporate personality	2
	(b) Explain the differences between public and private companies	2
	(c) Explain the purpose and legal status of the Articles of Association	2
	(d) Explain the main advantages and disadvantages of carrying on business through the medium of a company limited by shares	2

Exam Technique Overview

1   **The Best Approach to the CBA**

You're not likely to have a great deal of 'spare time' during the CBA itself so you must make sure you don't waste a single minute.

You should:

1.   Work through the whole exam, answering any questions you think you can answer correctly in a reasonably short time. If you find on occasion that you are not very confident with your answer, click the "Flag for Review" button before moving on.

2.   Click "Next" for any that have long scenarios or are very complex and return to these later.

3.   When you reach the 60th question, use the Review Screen to return to any questions you skipped past or any you flagged for review

Here's how the tools in the exam will help you to do this in a controlled and efficient way:

The 'Next' button

What does it do? This will move you on to the next question whether or not you have completed the one you are on.

When should I use it? Use this to move through the exam on your first pass through if you encounter a question that you suspect is going to take you a long time to answer. The Review Screen (see below) will help you to return to these questions later in the exam.

The 'Flag for Review' button

What does it do? This button will turn the icon yellow and when you reach the end of the exam questions you will be told that you have flagged specific questions for review. If the exam time runs out before you have reviewed any flagged questions then they will be submitted as they are.

When should I use it? Use this when you've answered a question but you're not completely comfortable with your answer. If there is time left at the end then you can quickly come back via the Review Screen (see below) but if time runs out at least it will submit your current answer. Do not use the Flag for Review button too often or you will end up with too long a list to review at the end. Important Note – scientific studies have shown that you are usually best to stick with your first instincts(!)

The Review Screen

What does it do? This screen appears after you click 'Next' on the 60th question. It shows you any Incomplete Questions and any you have Flagged for Review. It allows you to jump back to specific questions OR work through all your Incomplete Questions OR work through all your Flagged for Review Questions.

When should I use it? As soon as you've completed your first run through the exam and reached the 60th question. The very first thing to do is to work through

all your Incomplete Questions as they will all be marked as incorrect if you don't submit an answer for these in the remaining time. Importantly, this will also help to pick up any questions you thought you'd completed but didn't answer properly (eg you only picked two answer options in a multi-response question that required three answers to be selected). After you've submitted answers for all your Incomplete Questions you should use the Review Screen to work through all the questions you Flagged for Review.

2 The different Objective Test Question Types

Passing your CBA is all about demonstrating your understanding of the technical syllabus content. You will find this easier to do if you are comfortable with the different types of Objective Test Questions that you will encounter in the CBA, especially if you have a practised approach to each one.

You will find yourself continuously practising these styles of questions throughout your Objective Test programme. This way you will check and reinforce your technical knowledge at the same time as becoming more and more comfortable with your approach to each style of question.

Multiple choice

Standard multiple choice items provide four options. 1 option is correct and the other 3 are incorrect. Incorrect options will be plausible, so you should expect to have to use detailed, syllabus-specific knowledge to identify the correct answer rather than relying on common sense.

Multiple response

A multiple response item is the same as a multiple choice question, except more than one response is required. You will be told how many options you need to select.

Number entry

Number entry (or 'fill in the blank') questions require you to type a short numerical response. You should carefully follow the instructions in the question in terms of how to type your answer – eg the correct number of decimal places

Drag and drop

Drag and drop questions require you to drag a "token" onto a pre-defined area. These tokens can be images or text. This type of question is effective at testing the order of events, labelling a diagram or linking events to outcomes.

Hot spot

These questions require you to identify an area or location on an image by clicking on it. This is commonly used to identify a specific point on a graph or diagram.

Item set

2-4 questions all relating to the same short scenario. Each question will be 'standalone', such that your ability to answer subsequent questions in the set does not rely on getting the first one correct.

Key to icons

 Key term

A key definition which is important to be aware of for the assessment

 Activity

An example which allows you to apply your knowledge to the technique covered in the Course Book. The solution is provided at the end of the chapter

 Illustration

A worked example which can be used to review and see how an assessment question could be answered

 Assessment focus point

A high priority point for the assessment

The importance of ethics

Learning outcomes

Having studied this chapter you will be able to:

- Explain the nature of ethics and its application to society, business and the accountancy profession

- Apply the values and attitudes that provide professional accountants with a commitment to act in the public interest and with social responsibility

- Explain the need for a framework of laws, regulations and standards in business and their application and why CIMA and IFAC each have ethical codes

- Distinguish between detailed rules-based and framework/principles approaches to ethics

- Identify the ethical issues significant to organisations and how CIMA partners with strategic bodies to assist its members with ethical tensions/synergies

- Describe how personal and organisational policies and values promote behaviour

Syllabus context

Ethics is a huge area for accountants. The accounting scandals that engulfed Enron and WorldCom have led to a need for increased regulation and guidance within the accountancy profession. In this chapter, you will see the non-legal codes that have been developed to assist accountants and public servants.

Chapter overview

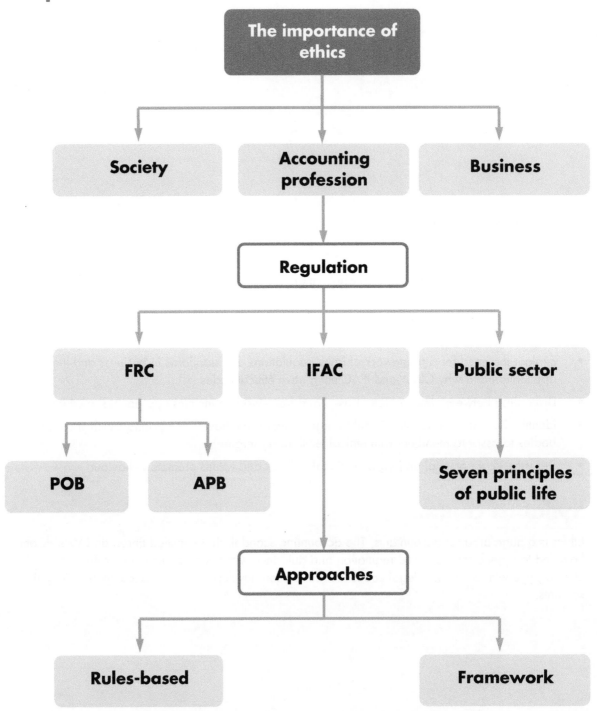

The importance of ethics

- Society
- Accounting profession
- Business

Regulation

- FRC
  - POB
  - APB
- IFAC
- Public sector
  - Seven principles of public life

Approaches

- Rules-based
- Framework

1 The importance of ethics

1.1 In order to qualify as a Chartered Management Accountant you will be expected to regard proper ethical behaviour in the same light as technical competence per CIMA's fundamental principles.

Key term

> **Ethics** can simply be defined as '**the science of morality**', or '**the difference between right and wrong**'. This extends to '**doing the right thing when no-one is watching**'.

1.2 Morals differ from ethics in that they relate to a person's individual beliefs, and are often derived from religious or cultural influences as opposed to national laws.

1.3 It is therefore possible to see ethical conflicts arise in situations where someone's actions are morally justifiable, despite being unethical and vice versa.

Illustration 1

Following a change in national law, John and Elton decide to get married. During their wedding preparations, John rang Harriet's Cakes to order a wedding cake, knowing that she specialises in bespoke cakes for grand occasions.

As John described how he wanted the cake to be decorated, Harriet became increasingly uncomfortable as she realised it would be to celebrate a same-sex marriage. Harriet informed John that whilst she wished him all the best for his forthcoming nuptials, she would be unable to supply him with a cake as her religious beliefs contradicted the recent change in the law.

In this instance, we see clear clash between Harriet's personal beliefs and the law. Her actions in refusing to supply a cake would constitute discrimination, and would be unlawful, despite her attempts to justify her unethical breach of law on the grounds of her personal morals.

Society

1.4 Many centuries ago, mankind discovered that the standard of living can be increased for all via mutual co-operation. Over time, this coexistence was formalised and regulated by the development of standards and principles, and today these are formalised in law.

1.5 Laws, however, set the minimum expectations for regulating the behaviour of our society, and tend to do so by prohibiting certain actions, such as theft and murder.

1.6 In a fair and civilised society, higher living standards and greater co-operation are often achieved by voluntarily exhibiting behaviour that exceeds the minimum requirements laid down by law eg by acting altruistically.

Illustration 2

The Charity Aid Foundation in the UK publishes an annual report on charitable giving. Some highlights from the 2015 report include:

- 79% of people gave money to charity in 2014
- People who donated monthly gave an average of £14 per month
- Total giving by adults was £10.4bn   (CAF UK Giving 2015)

Business

1.7 A relatively recent phenomenon is the acceptance that 'good ethics can be good business'. By this we mean that there can be a financial payback for companies that go above and beyond their minimum obligations.

1.8 Businesses must therefore develop their own ethical values, and these can sometimes be seen in their corporate mission statements, objectives, internal working practices as well as the products and service that they supply. For instance, it is now the industry norm for coffee shops to only sell 'fair trade' products.

1.9 Where businesses are found to have acted unethically, they breach the trust that society places in them, and this can have devastating effects on their reputations and consequently, their sales.

Illustration 3

Starbucks' sales tumbled in Britain in the wake of its tax-avoidance row. The coffee shop chain also came under attack as accounts showed it had kept in place a controversial offshore structure which wipes out profits in the UK.

The company said revenues fell by 3.4 per cent to £399.4m in the year to September 2013 from £413.4m a year earlier.

Accountancy profession

1.10 Professional accountants have a leadership role in society, and as such, society expects them to behave and act in the public interest. Incidents such as the collapse of Enron and WorldCom have severely dented public confidence in the accounting profession, further increasing the need for clear and ethical guidelines.

1.11 We will see in a later topic how CIMA regulates the affairs of its members, but here we can consider the key reasons why accountants should behave ethically.

- Ethical issues may also be a matter of law, so need to be followed.

- The profession is represented by each of its members, so relies on each and every one of them to uphold certain standards.

- An accountant's ethical behaviour serves to protect the public interest.

- The consequences of unethical behaviour impact, not only on the accountant's own career, but can jeopardise the jobs of others and endanger the reputation of the whole industry.

- Accountants employed in the public sector are duty-bound to protect tax-payers' money.

Activity 1: Ethics and business

Required

Which of the following statements is correct?

A   Good ethics is always good business.
B   Good ethics is often good business.
C   Good ethics is rarely good business.
D   Good ethics is never good business.

Solution

2 Regulation of professional ethics

2.1   The ethical framework for **accountants in the UK** has been provided by the Financial Reporting Council (**FRC**).

2.2   The FRC has two sub-bodies that monitor the accountability of the accounting profession:

(1)   **Codes and Standards Committee** – provides strategic input and leadership, considering and advising the FRC Board upon draft Codes and Standards and considers, and, comments upon proposed developments in relation to international Codes and Standards and regulation. It has three separate councils with specialisms in the following areas:

- Audit and Assurance Council
- Corporate Reporting Council
- Actuarial Council.

(2) **Conduct Committee** – responsible for overseeing the FRC's Conduct Division overseeing the monitoring of recognised supervisory bodies (such as CIMA), audit quality reviews, corporate reporting reviews, professional discipline and the oversight of the regulation of accountants and actuaries. It has three separate committees:

- Corporate Reporting Review Committee
- Audit Quality Review Committee
- Case Management Committee – dealing with disciplinary cases.

2.3 **Globally** the profession is regulated by the International Federation of Accountants (**IFAC**), which has a published code of ethics, compiled by The International Ethics Standards Board for Accountants (**IESBA**) covering:

- Integrity
- Objectivity
- Professional competence and due care
- Confidentiality
- Professional behaviour.

2.4 IFAC's role in regulation is to ensure consistent minimum standards in areas such as:

- **Education** – ensuring professional exams include compulsory subjects such as audit, accounting, law and economics

- **Examinations** – requiring exams to test application as well as theory

- **Experience** – requiring minimum level of professional experience to gain a chartered qualification.

Accountants in the public sector

2.5 **Public sector employees**, including accountants, are governed by the **'The Seven Principles of Public Life'** issues by the Committee of Standards in Public Life. These are listed below.

(a) **Leadership** – individuals must promote and respect the other principles
(b) **Honesty** – conflicts of interest must be declared
(c) **Objectivity** – appointments and contracts awarded on merit
(d) **Accountability** – individuals are responsible for their own actions
(e) **Integrity** – avoid actions which could unduly influence decision making
(f) **Selflessness** – individuals must always act solely in the public interest
(g) **Openness** – information on decision making must be made available.

The work of CIMA

2.6 CIMA partners with many strategic bodies to assist its members in dealing with ethical tensions/synergies. For instance, aside from publishing its own code of ethics (which you will see in the next Topic) and guidance on how to resolve ethical dilemmas, CIMA regularly runs **surveys**, **focus groups** and publishes its findings to assess the ethical standards of its members and affiliates.

2.7 Part of CIMA's work focuses on the concept of responsible business. CIMA define this as:

Key term

Responsible business	An organisation's commitment to operating in a way that is economically, socially and environmentally sustainable, and ensuring this prevails while still upholding the interests of its various stakeholder groups.

2.8 Within their research, CIMA regularly assesses for instance, whether partner organisations have:

- A statement of ethical values and principals
- Specific guidance on sensitive topics such as bribery
- Staff guidance on ethical compliance
- Training on ethical standards at work
- A hotline allowing employees to gain ethical advice
- Incentives for staff who uphold the organisation's ethical standards.

2.9 Organisational tools such as those laid-out above will assist businesses in aligning their values with those of their employees, and may be reflected in recruitment techniques, training resources, work place practices and the remuneration framework.

Activity 2: Principles of public life

Tony is a senior accountant at the Ministry of Health and whilst performing a routine review of the monthly expense accounts noticed some suspiciously large transactions being claimed by a colleague, Gordon. When confronted, Gordon broke down in tears and explained that he was 'borrowing money' to cover his children's school fees as his wife had recently lost her job due to ill health. Gordon promised that as soon as his wife recovered and found employment, he would pay the money back.

Required

Which of the following aspects of the Seven Principles of Public Life has Gordon breached?

Selflessness	☑
Integrity	☑
Objectivity	☐ ?
Accountability	☑
Openness	☐ ?
Honesty	☑
Leadership	☑

Solution

---

3 Rules-based and Framework approaches

Rules-based approach

3.1 Where accountants fail to successfully regulate their own behaviour, they face the risk of restrictive statutes being implemented, such as the **Sarbanes-Oxley Act** Corporate Governance legislation in the USA. This legislative approach is an example of what is known as the **'rules-based'** approach.

3.2 The rules-based (sometimes referred to as the **compliance**) approach has the following advantages and disadvantages.

Advantages	Disadvantages
Rules for specific outcomes	Long and lengthy rulebooks
Consistent application	Cannot learn every rule
Breaches easy to identify	Removes member discretion

Framework approach

3.3 By contrast, in the UK a voluntary '**framework**' approach to corporate governance has been adopted, driven by values and principles.

3.4 The framework (sometimes referred to as the **ethics-based**) approach has the following advantages and disadvantages.

Advantages	Disadvantages
Encourages proactive actions	Interpretations can be subjective
Treats members as individuals	Potential for inconsistency
Flexibility helps in complex situations	Ambiguity may be confusing
Harder to search for loopholes	Guidelines eventually become rules

Contrasting the approaches

Characteristic	Rules-based	Framework
Enforceability	Mandatory	Discretionary
Choices	Obedience	Judgement
Standards	Explicit	Implicit
Motivation	Fear-driven	Values-driven
Approach	Law-based	Principles-based
Objective	Detection	Prevention
Measure	Rules	Principles (values)

Activity 3: Ethical approaches

Required

Match these words to the appropriate approach

A   Letter of the law — *Rules*
B   Black and white — *Rules*
C   Discretion — *framework*
D   Guidelines — *framework*
E   Flexible — *framework*
F   Compliance — *Rules*

Solution

Rules-based	Framework

Chapter summary

- Humans have developed a framework of **rules** to regulate behaviour – the law. However, **ethics** are a set of **moral principles** that guide behaviour.

- Individuals have ethical values and beliefs about what constitutes 'right' and 'wrong' behaviour. These values often reflect those of the individual's family, culture and educational environment they are brought up in.

- Ethics are **not the same** thing as the law or the rules of religion.

- As an accountant, your values and attitudes flow through everything that you do professionally. They contribute to the **trust** the wider community puts in the profession and the perception it has of it.

- Professional institutions (such as **CIMA**) have an overriding duty to protect the **public interest**. To ensure members act in a manner which achieves this, most have developed **codes of conduct** to guide their behaviour.

- CIMA, along with the other UK accounting bodies are regulated by the Financial Reporting Council (**FRC**). The two sub-bodies of the FRC that specifically regulate accountants are, the **Codes and Standards Committee** and, the **Conduct Committee.**

- CIMA is affiliated to the International Federation of Accountants (**IFAC**) is an international body representing all the major accountancy bodies across the world. Its mission is to develop the high standards of professional accountants and enhance the quality of services they provide.

- Approaches to ethics can be based upon **rules** or **frameworks**. These contrasting approaches differ in the respect to which they encourage adherence to strict and comprehensive **rule books**, as opposed to more flexible and discretionary **guidelines**.

Keywords

- **Ethics:** can simply be defined as 'the science of morality', or 'the difference between right and wrong'. This extends to 'doing the right thing when no-one is watching'.

- **Responsible business:** An organisation's commitment to operating in a way that is economically, socially and environmentally sustainable, and ensuring this prevails while still upholding the interests of its various stakeholder groups.

Activity answers

Activity 1: Ethics and business

B   Good ethics is often good business. Good ethics is generally good for business, so C and D are incorrect. It is not true, however, to say it is *always* good for business, so A is incorrect too.

Activity 2: Principles of public life

Gordon's theft has resulted in multiple breaches of his duties:

- Selflessness – failed to act solely in the public interest

- Integrity – placed himself in a position where finances affected his performance of his public duty

- Accountability – Gordon is accountable for the money he has stolen

- Honesty – theft by definition is the dishonest appropriation of property belonging to another with the intention to permanently deprive

- Leadership – this is automatically breached when any of the other six duties are not upheld.

Objectivity is not relevant as there is no suggestion of improper contractual awards. Openness is not relevant as no information has been withheld.

Activity 3: Ethical approaches

Rules-based	Framework
Letter of the law	Discretion
Black and white	Guidelines
Compliance	Flexible

1   Behaving ethically is the minimum level of behaviour expected of an individual by society.

    True ☐

    False ☑

2   Which **TWO** of the following are both sub-bodies of the Conduct Committee of the Financial Reporting Council?

    (A)   Corporate Reporting Review Committee
    (B)   Audit and Assurance Committee *Council*
    C   Actuarial Committee *Council*
    (D)   Case Management Committee

3   If an organisation's code of conduct is in conflict with the law, the legal position will prevail.

    True ☑

    False ☐

4   The Committee of Standards in Public Life set out seven principles that individuals employed in the public sector should follow. Which of the following are included in these principles.

    Select **all** that apply.

    ✓ A   Selflessness
    ✓ B   Openness
      C   Professionalism
    ✓ D   Objectivity

5   How does a framework-based approach to a code of ethics differ from a rules-based approach?

    A   A rules-based approach is based around general principles.

    (B)   A framework-based approach prescribes general guidelines on how to handle certain situations.

    C   A rules-based approach is designed to cope with constantly evolving circumstances.

    D   A framework-based approach requires members to learn specific rules covering every conceivable situation.

CIMA's code of ethics

2

Learning outcomes

Having studied this chapter you will be able to:

- Explain the need to develop the virtues of reliability, responsibility, timeliness, courtesy and respect

- Explain the fundamental ethical principles

- Identify concepts of independence, scepticism, accountability and social responsibility

- Illustrate the threats and safeguards to the fundamental ethical principles

Syllabus context

Having learned what ethics is in the previous chapter, we now focus on what this means as a practising accountant. You will learn how CIMA regulates the affairs of its members via its Ethical Code, and what threats there are to this code. You will then move onto looking at the personal and professional qualities expected of a CIMA member, and how CPD and lifelong learning ensure that you continue to meet these standards throughout your career.

Chapter overview

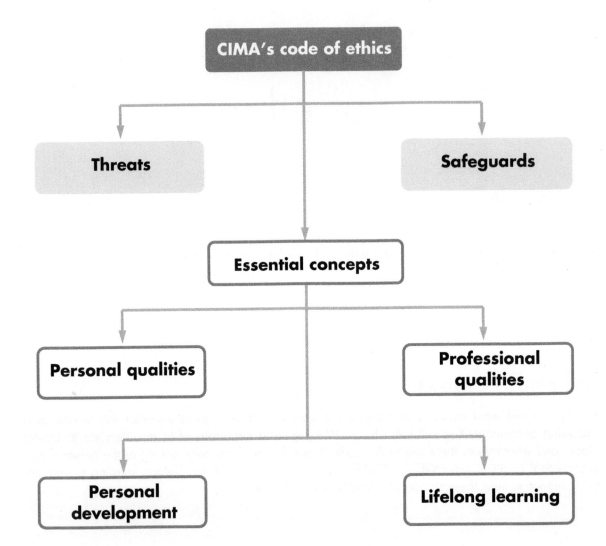

1 CIMA Code of Ethics

1.1 Professional institutions such as CIMA have an overriding duty to protect the public interest. To ensure their members act in a manner which achieves this, they have developed codes of conduct to guide members' behaviour.

1.2 The CIMA Code of Ethics identifies **five fundamental principles** and is based upon a framework approach relying on trust and self-regulation, rather than strict enforcement of rules.

Key term

Objectivity	**refers** to the ability to make judgements and decisions **free from bias**, and within this the guidelines also make it clear that you are expected to avoid situations that cause a **conflict of interest** to arise.
Professional competence and due care	means that an accountant should only take on tasks for which they are **technically competent** to perform. There is also a duty to **take reasonable care** and remain **technically up-to-date**.
Professional behaviour	means not doing anything that will discredit CIMA or the wider accounting profession. This is defined as 'actions which a reasonable and informed third party, having knowledge of all relevant information, would conclude negatively affects the good reputation of the profession'.
Integrity	means that an individual acts in a manner that is **honest** and **straightforward** in all professional and business relationships. This extends beyond the work that an accountant produces, and extends to the manner in which they **conduct** themselves.
Confidentiality	means having a duty to safeguard any information in your possession unless there is a legal or professional duty to disclose. This is an area that strays from ethics into law and in order to bring clarity to this area, CIMA has provided a list of examples where confidential information can be disclosed:

(a) When permitted by law
(b) When permitted by the client or employer
(c) When required by law
(d) When permitted by a professional duty or right.

Illustration 1

Samantha is the group accountant working for the Whizz Formula 1 team. Having been offered a job by a rival team, Samantha downloaded some sensitive technical data from the Whizz servers whilst working her notice period. When Whizz noticed similarities between their own car and Samantha's new team, they reviewed their server records and discovered the precise time of the data leak. Whilst they suspect Samantha took the data, they are unable to prove anything as Samantha had logged into someone else's machine and used her boss's passwords.

In this case Samantha has committed several breaches of the CIMA code. Quite obviously she has breached the confidentiality clause, but aside from this, she has demonstrated a lack of objectivity by placing herself in a conflict of interests. Stealing data also shows a lack of professional behaviour as well as a lack of integrity.

Activity 1: Donald

Donald's company is moving offices. During the move he finds his computer (which contains the payroll budgets) has been moved and he will not have access to it for a couple of days. The human resources director has requested information from the budgets for an important meeting today. Donald thinks he can remember the information but is not 100% sure of it.

Required

What should Donald do?

- A   Refuse to provide the information.
- B   Provide the information from memory.
- C   Provide the information with a disclaimer on its accuracy.
- D   Make an educated guess and provide an update later.

Solution

1.3 The Code itself is split into three parts.

(a) **General Application** – an introduction to the five fundamental principles

(b) Professional Accountants in **Public Practice** – covering the specific issues relevant to public practice, including conflicts of interest, fees, gifts and objectivity

(c) Professional Accountants in **Business** – covering specific issues such as preparation and reporting of information

2 Threat and safeguards

2.1 The threat to professional ethics have been identified as:

(a) **Self-interest** – the threat that a financial/other interest will inappropriately influence the accountant's judgment or behaviour

(b) **Self-review** – the threat that a professional accountant will not appropriately evaluate the results of a previous judgment made or activity or service performed by the professional accountant, or by another individual within the professional accountant's firm

(c) **Advocacy** – the threat that a professional accountant will promote a client's or employer's position to the point that the professional accountant's objectivity is compromised

(d) **Familiarity** – the threat that due to a long or close relationship with a client or employer, a professional accountant will be too sympathetic to their interests or too accepting of their work

(e) **Intimidation** – the threat that a professional accountant will be deterred from acting objectively because of actual or perceived pressures, including attempts to exercise undue influence over the professional accountant.

2.2 To help overcome these threats CIMA have identified the following safeguards:

- Education and training
- Requiring members follow the CPD pathway
- Corporate governance requirements
- Professional standards
- Professional or regulatory monitoring and disciplinary procedures
- External review by a legally empowered third party of the reports, returns, communications or information produced by a professional accountant.

Activity 2: Ethical threats

Which of the following is a threat to the ethics of an accountant?

A   The UK code of Corporate Governance.

B   Attendance at CPD courses.

C   External review.

D   Familiarity.

Solution

3 Essential concepts

3.1   Aside from the need to promote ethical behaviour CIMA provides guidance on the virtues they expect of their members. These virtues are reflected in the following **personal qualities**:

    (a)   **Reliability** – you should be trustworthy and dependable

    (b)   **Responsibility** – you should take ownership for your actions and decisions

    (c)   **Respect** – you should develop constructive relationships, and this involves listening and understanding other people's points of view

    (d)   **Timeliness** – being able to work within agreed timeframes

    (e)   **Courtesy** – conducting yourself with courtesy, consideration and good manners

3.2   Additionally there are professional qualities which must be exhibited too:

    (a)   **Independence of mind** – being able to act with integrity and professional scepticism, and **independence in appearance** – do third parties consider you to be independent of mind?

    (b)   **Professional scepticism** – questioning the veracity of information provided to you

(c) **Accountability** – being responsible and answerable for your actions

(d) **Social responsibility** – the individual as a stakeholder in society must behave with integrity, courtesy, respect and due care

---

Illustration 2

Accountants should be aware that their work may affect their company's stakeholders or the public in some way. Examples include:

* **Audit work** – the public rely on audited accounts as a control to ensure that accounts are generally free from material errors

* **Accountancy work** – the accurate preparation of accounts is essential for assessing levels of profitability and taxation

* **Investment decisions** – accurate investment analysis such as NPV calculations are used to ensure investor's money is wisely invested

---

Activity 3: Independence

Independence is an important quality for accountants to demonstrate when providing assurance services. The two key elements of independence are:

A   Mind and appearance
B   Thought and appearance
C   Mind and thought
D   None of the above

Solution

4 Personal development and lifelong learning

4.1   In order to ensure that you are able to constantly discharge your professional obligations, CIMA have a **Professional Development Cycle**. This ensure that their members engage in:

Key term

Professional Development	'The development of personal qualities such as communication skills, assertiveness, time management and relationship building. They are skills that have to be developed by an individual and must come from deep within them.'
Lifelong learning	'The concept that an individual never stops learning and should be open to new ideas, decisions, skills and behaviours.'

4.2 The stages in the CIMA professional development cycle are:

(a) **Define** – members should define their current and desired roles

(b) **Assess** – current capabilities and competences to identify knowledge gaps used to create learning objectives

(c) **Design** – members should construct an activity programme

(d) **Act** – members should undertake learning activities

(e) **Reflect** – activities should be reflected upon to assess if further training is needed

(f) **Evaluate** – any remaining gaps should be rolled into the next cycle.

4.3 The following activities count as development:

(a) Reading professional publications
(b) Computer-based training
(c) Research and project work
(d) Attending CIMA events.

Activity 4: Technical awareness

Accountants must stay technically up to date because the public expects them to.

True ☑
False ☐

Solution

Chapter summary

- CIMA's ethical guidelines give the fundamental principles that members should follow in their professional lives. The principles are consistent with the IFAC code including:

    - Objectivity
    - Professional competence and due care
    - Professional behaviour
    - Integrity
    - Confidentiality.

- The threats to ethics are:

    - Self-interest
    - Self-review
    - Advocacy
    - Familiarity
    - Intimidation.

- The personal qualities that an accountant should demonstrate are:

    - Reliability
    - Responsibility
    - Timeliness
    - Courtesy
    - Respect.

- The professional qualities an accountant should demonstrate are:

    - Independence
    - Scepticism
    - Accountability
    - Social responsibility.

- Personal development is the development of personal qualities such as communication skills, assertiveness, time management and relationship building. They are skills that have to be developed by an individual and must come from deep within them.

- The professional development cycle has the following stages: define, assess, design, act, reflect, evaluate.

- Lifelong learning is the concept that an individual never stops learning and should be open to new ideas, decisions, skills or behaviours.

- **Confidentiality:** means having a duty to safeguard any information in your possession unless there is a legal or professional duty to disclose. This is an area that strays from ethics into law and in order to bring clarity to this area, CIMA has provided a list of examples where confidential information can be disclosed:

  (a)   When permitted by law
  (b)   When permitted by the client or employer
  (c)   When required by law
  (d)   When permitted by a professional duty or right.

- **Integrity:** means that an individual acts in a manner that is honest and straightforward in all professional and business relationships. This extends beyond the work that an accountant produces, and extends to the manner in which they conduct themselves.

- **Lifelong learning**: 'The concept that an individual never stops learning and should be open to new ideas, decisions, skills and behaviours.'

- **Objectivity:** refers to the ability to make judgements and decisions free from bias, and within this the guidelines also make it clear that you are expected to avoid situations that cause a conflict of interest to arise.

- **Professional behaviour:** means not doing anything that will discredit CIMA or the wider accounting profession. This is defined as 'actions which a reasonable and informed third party, having knowledge of all relevant information, would conclude negatively affects the good reputation of the profession'.

- **Professional competence and due care:** means that an accountant should only take on tasks for which they are technically competent to perform. There is also a duty to take reasonable care and remain technically up-to-date.

- **Professional Development:** 'The development of personal qualities such as communication skills, assertiveness, time management and relationship building. They are skills that have to be developed by an individual and must come from deep within them.'

Activity answers

Activity 1: Donald

A   Donald should not make himself party to inaccurate information. Options B and C potentially make him party to such misinformation. Option D could mean him breaking the principle of due care by rushing a calculation.

Activity 2: Ethical threats

D   Familiarity is one of the five threats to ethics – the other options are safeguards.

Activity 3: Independence

B   Act follows design. The order is Define, Assess, Design, Act, Reflect, Evaluate

Activity 4: Technical awareness

True – public expectation has driven the need for CPD within the accounting profession.

1   Which of the following are fundamental principles in CIMA's ethical guidelines?

   (i)   Confidentiality
   (ii)   Scepticism
   (iii) Integrity
   (iv)   Independence

   A   (i) and (ii) only
   B   (i), (ii) and (iii) only
   C   (i) and (iii) only
   D   All of the above

2   List five personal qualities expected of an accountant.

   (i)   R...*eliability*
   (ii)   R...*esponsibility*
   (iii) T...*imely*
   (iv)   C...*ourtesy*
   (v)   R...*espect*

3   Which stage follows Design in CIMA's professional development cycle?

   A   Define
   B   Act
   C   Reflect
   D   Evaluate

4   Which statement describes the ethical principle of integrity?

   A   The principle of straightforwardness and honesty in all dealings
   B   The principle of freedom from conflicts of interest – *Objectivity*
   C   The principle of ensuring work is as accurate as possible – *Prof Competence*
   D   The principle of maintaining security of information – *Confidentiality*

5   Which statement describes the ethical principle of objectivity?

   A   The principle of avoiding situations that may discredit the profession

   B   The principle of ensuring you are capable of performing the work

   C   The principle of impartiality and avoiding the influence of others whilst working

   D   The principle of avoiding the use of information obtained in the course of work for your own advantage

Ethical dilemmas

3

Learning outcomes

Having studied this chapter you will be able to:

- Explain the relationship between the CIMA Code of Ethics and the law
- Describe the consequences of ethical behaviour to society, business, the profession and the professional accountant
- Identify conflicting perspectives of interest when dealing with stakeholders in society, business and the values of professional accountants
- Identify situations where ethical dilemmas and conflicts of interest occur, based on CIMA's ethical checklist

Syllabus context

In the previous chapter, we looked at the concept of ethics, and how CIMA regulates the ethical conduct of its members. In this chapter, we look at the wider importance of ethical behaviour for organisations, and how individuals can deal with ethical dilemmas.

Chapter overview

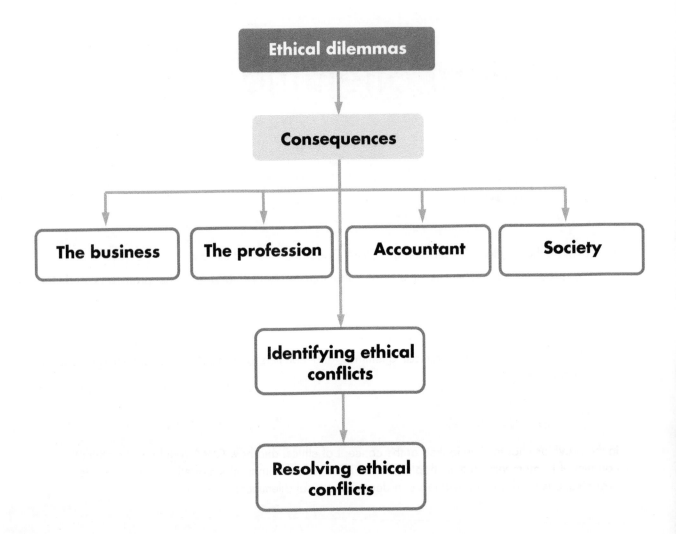

1 Consequences of unethical behaviour

1.1 When considering the consequences of unethical behaviour it is sensible to start by considering the relationship between the CIMA Code of Ethics and the law.

1.2 The CIMA Code is a **law of the institute**, and therefore any breach of the Code can give rise to disciplinary action. However the Code is not part of national law, and therefore will not automatically give rise to civil or criminal actions, though these *could* follow.

Illustration 1

Frank is a CGMA working for Lennox Ltd. Frank has been put in charge of finalising construction contracts for a new warehouse, and uses this position to negotiate some 'kickbacks' for himself with certain suppliers. In one instance, Frank agreed to accept a tender for building materials that was 10% higher than an equivalent quote of £500,000 on the understanding that Frank would receive an undeclared cash payment of half of the difference.

In this instance, Frank has breached the CIMA code with respect to objectivity, integrity, confidentiality and professional behaviour. He therefore faces disciplinary action from CIMA that could result in his expulsion from the institute. Aside from this, Frank's actions could lead to a criminal prosecution under the Bribery Act, so he faces prison and/or a fine; the undeclared payments may also lead to action from the tax authorities. Finally, Lennox Ltd would be justified in dismissing Frank, and could take civil action to recover any amounts they have overpaid as a result of the unlawful awarding of contracts.

1.3 The illustration above highlights the potential interaction between the CIMA Code, the national law and an individual's employment contract.

1.4 The consequences of unethical behaviour by organisations and their employees can be far reaching:

The Accountant

1.5 An unethical accountant risks the following if their unethical behaviour is discovered:

- Being subject to a professional disciplinary hearing

- Being fined or being struck off as an accountant

- Losing their job, either through an employer disciplinary hearing or being unable to practice

- Their actions becoming public knowledge and their personal reputation damaged

- Prosecution if the behaviour is criminal

- Being sued for damages by an affected party.

The Accountancy Profession

1.6 Accountants have a high degree of trust placed on them by society. Therefore any high profile, or repeated breaches can have severe consequences for the whole profession. These may include:

- Loss of reputation
- Reduced employability of accountants
- Pressure by outside bodies to tighten up regulations and penalties
- Government intervention if it is thought the profession is incapable of self-regulation
- Accountancy bodies losing their 'chartered' status.

The Business

1.7 If a business knowingly acts unethically, or allows its employees to breach ethical codes, they face the following risks:

- Loss of reputation and therefore sales/contracts
- Threat of legal action or investigation by regulators
- Resignation of key ethically-minded staff
- Business closure, resulting in redundancy.

Society as a whole

1.8 Given that society relies upon the work of accountants to assess the profitability of organisations and their liability for tax, there are consequences for the wider society of unethical behaviour.

- The work of all accountants would be called into question.
- Unethical companies would eventually fail as they would lose public confidence.
- The financial markets would be affected if investors could not rely on audit reports and financial statements.
- The tax authorities may question tax computations, affecting the amount of tax collected.
- Criminals may gravitate towards the profession to make money from fraud or other financial crime.
- Commercial organisations would not function if they were unable rely on their accountants' work.

Illustration 2

The notorious 'rogue trading' of Nick Leeson caused the collapse of Barings Bank in 1995 with debts of over £800m. Slack internal controls allowed Leeson to enter into a series of unhedged trades that went wrong, racking up huge losses that resulted in the world's oldest merchant bank being sold for a notional £1 to the Dutch Bank, ING. ING took on the Barings name, but little else.

Investors in Baring's lost millions, many employees lost their jobs and Leeson spent four years in a Singapore prison. In response to this, and other high profile scandals, the UK started to review its existing corporate governance frameworks.

Activity 1: CIMA code of ethics

Which of the following statements is correct?

Required

A   The CIMA Code of Ethics has the power of law.
B   The CIMA Code of Ethics is the law of CIMA.
C   Breaches of the CIMA Code of Ethics are assessed in court.
D   The CIMA Code of Ethics differs from country to country.

Solution

2   Identifying ethical conflicts

2.1 Ethical conflicts arise in situations where two values or requirements seem to be incompatible. They can also arise where two conflicting demands or obligations are placed on an individual.

2.2 Ethical conflicts can occur as a result of tensions between four sets of values:

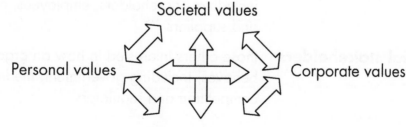

Societal values

Personal values

Corporate values

Professional values

2.3 **Societal values** – the obligations imposed by national law and customs

2.4 **Personal values** – the values and principles held by the individual

2.5 **Corporate values** – the values and principles of the organisation where the employee works, often laid down in a corporate ethical code

2.6 **Professional values** – the values and principles of the professional body that the individual is a member of, again laid down in ethical codes.

2.7 Aside from these, contractual obligations can add an additional layer of complexity.

Illustration 3

Societal values and corporate values

An individual may be asked by their employer to act in an illegal way, for example, to discriminate against a disabled or ethnic minority employee.

Personal values and corporate values

An individual may not agree with certain activities of their organisation, such as the use of child labour in foreign factories. Whilst not necessarily illegal, it goes against their own moral beliefs.

Professional values and corporate values

An individual is put into a position by their employer where they are required to amend a set of accounts to improve the profit figure. Such amendments go against the code of conduct of their accountancy body.

Contractual obligations

An interim chief executive has a clause entitling them to 10% of the value of any savings they can make over a six-month period. Having clashed several times with a high-level manager, they could make that person redundant and receive cash to the value of 10% of the salary saved.

2.8 A source of ethical tension can be the contrasting demands of **stakeholders**. Broadly speaking all organisations are deemed to have two types of stakeholders:

Key term

Financial stakeholders	those groups that would directly suffer if something happened to an organisation, including, shareholders, employees, customers and suppliers
Non-financial stakeholders	those others interested in how an organisation behaves, including government, media, competition and regulators.

2.9 Practical examples of ethical dilemmas arising include:

- Pressure from an overbearing colleague or from family or friends

- Members asked to act contrary to technical and/or professional standards

- Divided loyalties between colleagues and professional standards

- Publication of misleading information

- Members having to do work beyond their degree of expertise or the experience they possess

- Personal relationships with other employees or clients

- Gifts and hospitality being offered.

2.10 Stakeholder conflict can also occur due to differing perspectives eg shareholders may be broadly focused on financial returns, whereas employees will be looking for job security, pay rises and training, as well as career advancement opportunities.

Activity 2: Values

Which of the following obligations are imposed by national laws?

Required

A   Professional values
B   Personal values
C   Corporate values
D   Societal values

Solution

3   Resolving ethical dilemmas

3.1 The general approach to resolving ethical issues is given by following CIMA's ethical checklist.

(1) **Check all the facts** – identify and document where possible. Do not rely on word of mouth

(2) **Is it ethical?** – have all of the ethical issues been considered? Refer to the CIMA Code of Ethics

(3) **Decide if the issue is legal in nature** – reference against national laws and professional standards

(4) **Identify any Fundamental Principles engaged** – refer to the CIMA Code –OPPIC

(5) **Identify any affected parties** – individuals, organisations, wider stakeholders

(6) **Consider possible courses of action** – escalate internally, seek professional legal advice or contact professional body/regulator

(7) **Seek professional/legal advice** – CIMA's ethics helpline, beware of confidentiality/whistleblowing regulations

(8) **Refuse to be associated with the conflict** – move departments, resign or seek legal advice.

3.2 When dealing with such matters, the organisation should try and ensure:

(a) **Transparency** – do you feel comfortable about the decision made, are your actions justifiable?

(b) **Effect** – have all affected parties been considered, all stakeholders considered?

(c) **Fairness** – would a rational bystander consider the outcomes to be fair?

Activity 3: Resolving conflict

What should a solution to an ethical conflict be?

A   Acceptable to the employer
B   Authorised by CIMA
C   Expressly permitted in IFAC's ethical code
D   Consistent with fundamental principles

Solution

Chapter summary

- Unethical behaviour will have consequences for:
    - You as an accountant
    - The accountancy profession
    - Society as a whole.

- Ethical conflicts are situations where two ethical values or requirements seem to be incompatible. They can also arise where two conflicting demands or obligations are placed upon you.

- A conflict of interest arises where you have a duty to two or more parties. Whilst working, information or other matters may arise that mean you cannot continue work for one party without harming another.

- Ethical conflicts may rise from:
    - Pressure from an overbearing colleague or from family or friends
    - Being asked to act contrary to technical and/or professional standards
    - Divided loyalties between colleagues and professional standards
    - Publication of misleading information
    - Having to do work beyond your degree of expertise/experience you possess
    - Personal relationships with other employees or clients
    - Gifts and hospitality being offered.

Keywords

- **Financial stakeholders:** those groups that would directly suffer if something happened to an organisation, including, shareholders, employees, customers and suppliers

- **Non-financial stakeholders:** those others interested in how an organisation behaves, including government, media, competition and regulators.

Activity answers

Activity 1: CIMA code of ethics

B   The CIMA Code of Ethics is the law of CIMA is correct. CIMA's code is not part of national law, and breaches are assessed internally, not in court. The Code is a global entity - there are no regional variants.

Activity 2: Values

D   Societal values – the obligations imposed by national law and customs.

Activity 3: Resolving conflict

D   Any solution must be consistent with fundamental ethical principles. They do not have to be authorised by CIMA or expressly permitted in IFAC's code. An ethical solution may be unacceptable to an employer who is behaving unethically.

1   Corporate values are the values and principles of the organisation where an individual works. They may be set out in ethical codes.

   True   [✓]
   False [ ]

2   Jack works for a large organisation as head of the accounts department. The company has recently introduced a policy which discriminates against disabled people during the recruitment process. Jack has no moral objections to the policy and applied it when he recently filled a vacancy in his department.

   This is an example of ethical tensions between which sets of values?

   A   Professional and corporate
   B   Personal and corporate
   C   Societal and corporate
   D   None – there are no ethical tensions in the scenario

3   Statutory obligations differ from contractual obligations, as fulfilling them is voluntary.

   True   [ ]
   False [✓]

4   Being objective as an accountant is an example of a:

   A   Societal value
   B   Professional value
   C   Corporate value
   D   Contractual obligation

5   CIMA has an ethical hotline which students and members can use to access help with any ethical issues they may face.

   True   [✓]
   False [ ]

The meaning of governance

4

Learning outcomes

Having studied this chapter you will be able to:

- Describe corporate governance

- Explain the interaction of corporate governance with business ethics and company law

- Explain the purpose, definition of the Organisation for Economic Co-operation and Development (OECD) principles of corporate governance

- Describe IFAC's main drivers of sustainable corporate success

- Illustrate CIMA's practical proposals for better corporate governance

- Distinguish between the detailed rules-based approach and principles-based approaches to governance

Syllabus context

Corporate governance is an increasingly important consideration for those that invest in, and those that direct companies. As a result of numerous high-profile corporate scandals, national governments have enacted corporate governance codes; some legal, others extra-legal. To ensure global consistency, the OECD has published a framework that acts as a benchmark.

Chapter overview

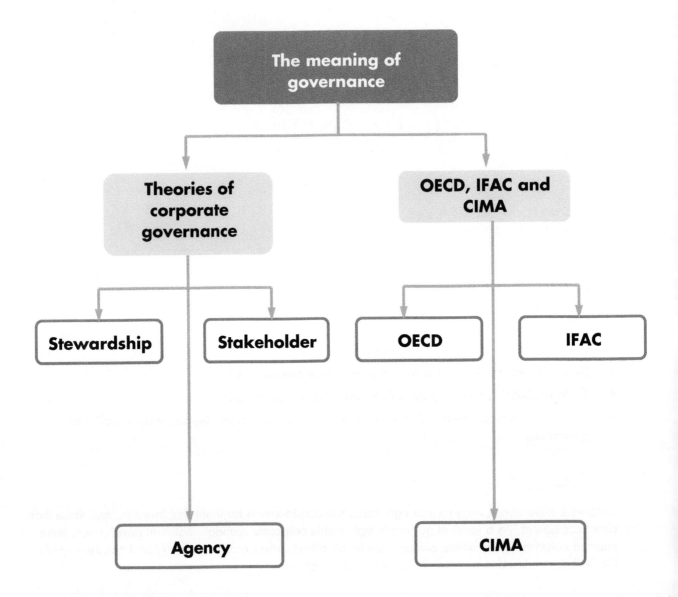

1 Corporate Governance

Key term

Corporate Governance is the system by which organisations are directed and controlled. Running an organisation of any type requires no specific qualifications, and there is no 'rule book', corporate governance aims to fill this gap.

1.1 The general aims of any system of corporate governance include:

   (a) Managing a **reduction in risk**

   (b) Setting **best practice guidelines**

   (c) Providing an **ethical** and **effective** management framework

   (d) Creating a willingness to **follow the spirit**, as well as the letter, of the framework

   (e) Building **accountability** for executive management.

1.2 Corporate governance is needed as numerous high profile scandals have dented market trust in the way large organisations are run, and without investor trust, organisations will find it hard and expensive to raise new finance.

1.3 The common themes of organisations that have failed due to poor governance included:

   (a) Dominant board members
   (b) Weak boards
   (c) Lack of stakeholder interaction
   (d) Lack of internal controls
   (e) Corporate greed, allied with stock market pressure for better results.

Illustration 1

Enron was once the world's sixth largest energy company, with its shares peaking at $90.75 in August 2000. By January 2002, the shares had fallen to $0.67. The extraordinary growth of Enron over the previous seven years was largely fuelled by a series of elaborate deceptions, made possible by exploiting accounting standards, with the complicity of the company's auditors, Arthur Anderson. The most damaging deception was the practice of hiding multi-billion pound loses in so called 'off balance sheet vehicles'. These entities were subsidiary companies that were legally controlled in such a way that they were not consolidated into Enron's group accounts. The company was therefore able to transfer losses into these companies, thus hiding them from investors.

In the year before the deception came to light, Enron paid its two most senior executives $67m and $42m. In the months before the company crashed, many senior executives sold their shareholdings in the company, something that ordinary employees were forbidden from doing by stock market regulations, and consequently, many lost their life savings. To compound matters, many employees had pension funds that only invested in Enron shares, leaving their retirement plans in tatters.

The fall-out from Enron was huge. Several top executives were imprisoned, Arthur Anderson collapsed and the US Government enacted the Sarbanes-Oxley Act

Stewardship theory

Key term

> **Stewardship theory** views the management of an organisation as its stewards, tasked with managing its assets in line with the wishes of the owners.

1.4 Should owners not be happy with the performance of the stewards, they should be dismissed. Stewardship theory therefore requires investors to take an **active interest** in the affairs of the organisation.

Stakeholder theory

Key term

> The **stakeholder theory** takes a more organic view of an organisation that goes beyond mere stewardship and states that the management has a duty of care not just to the owners, but also to the wider stakeholder community.

Agency theory

Key term

> **Agency theory** views the managers of an organisation as acting in an agency capacity, seeking to **service their own self-interest**, and looking after the performance of the company only to the extent where this promotes their own interests. This gives rise to the **agency problem**.

1.5 The agency problem arises from the fact that there is a separation of ownership and management. In effect, the directors are responsible for forming contractual relationships with third parties on behalf of the company, as illustrated below.

| Third parties (stakeholders) | Agents (directors) | Principal (company) |

Customer

Bank

Supplier

Company

1.6 The agency problem can give rise to circumstances where the directors may well be placed in positions where conflicts of interest arise; where doing what is best for the company is not what is best for themselves personally eg where a merger will result in a director receiving a substantial pay-off for losing their job, they may recommend this, even if it's not in their company's best interests.

Activity 1: Stakeholder theory

Which of the following statements is correct?

Required

A   Agency theory encourages directors to act in the company's best interests.

B   Stakeholder theory views the directors as stewards of the company.

C   Corporate governance codes aim to empower CEOs to overcome weak boards.

D   Stakeholder theory views companies as entities that owe a duty of care to the wider community.

Solution

2 Ethics, law and governance

2.1 We have seen previously that ethics is the science of 'right and wrong', and that these differ from morals which are derived from an individual's personal beliefs. Together, these lead to norms that society **expects** people to follow.

2.2 Laws, on the other hand, are obligations placed upon individuals by legislators and judges, and as such, **must be obeyed**.

2.3 Corporate governance generally sits in the gap between these eg they are an additional set of rules and guidance for organisations. They can be said to be bridging the gap between the minimum standards that the law demands, balancing this with the socially responsible standards that society expects. There are, however, some important exceptions, such as the Sarbanes-Oxley Act in the USA, which is part of the national law and thus imposes legal standards.

Illustration 2

Marks and Spencer plc is one of Britain's largest and most well-known companies. As part of a turnaround plan Stuart Rose was appointed as the CEO in 2004, and after some success he was elevated to the role of CEO and Chairman in 2008. This sparked an investor backlash, as combining these roles is contrary to the best practice advised in the UK Code of Corporate Governance. Whilst M&S had broken no laws this breach of UK governance upset investors to the degree that many large investors voted against his Chairmanship at the next AGM. Rose stepped down as CEO in 2010, a year ahead of schedule in an effort to appease angry investors.

2.4 There is some significant overlap between governance and law. For instance, the executives of Enron were imprisoned as their actions were illegal and unethical. Aside from criminality, there are a number of legal regulations that bind company behaviour, and a failure to follow this would constitute poor governance.

2.5 The main legal regulations in the UK are:

(a) Companies Act – regulates a wide range of company actions
(b) Company Directors Disqualification Act – regulates director's conduct
(c) Criminal Justice Act – regulates insider dealing
(d) Insolvency Act – regulates administration and insolvency
(e) UK Listing Authority Rules – rules on gaining and maintaining a listing.

Activity 2: Corporate governance

Robert is the CEO of a major listed media company which he founded. Desperate to prop-up the company's fading share price, he ordered Rupert, the Finance Director, to withdraw £500m from the company's pension fund. Rupert was too scared of Robert to object, so reluctantly went along with this. Robert used this money to buy 100m shares in the company on behalf of the pension fund in the company at £5 each - they were previously trading at £4.20. At the end of this intervention, the company's share price rose to £4.80.

Required

Which of the following statements is correct. Tick all that apply

Robert's actions are an example of strong management. ☐

Rupert was correct to carry out the instruction of the CEO. ☐

The governance within the company appears to be weak. ☐

Robert's actions are correct but unethical. ☐

Solution

2.6 As with ethical codes there is a choice between a principles and rules-based approach to governance. Some of the advantages of these contrasting approaches are presented below.

Principles	Rules-based
Co's regulated already	Guides useless without rules
Rules approach is costly	100% compliance = good governance
Co's can't all follow the same rules	Compliance cost < cost of error / fraud
Co's may have valid exemptions	Principles relies upon active shareholders

3 OECD, IFAC and CIMA

3.1 The Organisation for Economic Co-Operation and Development first published their principles of corporate governance in 1999. This non-binding code aims to act as a benchmark to ensure that national codes all comply with generally accepted best practice. The six principles identified are:

(a) **Ensuring the basis for an effective corporate governance framework** – emphasising the role of corporate governance in promoting transparent and fair markets and efficient allocation of resources

(b) **The rights and equitable treatment of shareholders and key ownership functions** – basic shareholder rights, the right to information, and the use of technology in shareholder communication

(c) **Institutional investors, stock markets and other intermediaries** – addressing the need for sound economic incentives through the investment chain, and the need for disclosure of conflicts of interest which may compromise the integrity of market makers and ratings agencies

(d) **The role of stakeholders in corporate governance** – outlines the benefits of active co-operation between corporations and stakeholders

(e) **Disclosure and transparency** – identifies the key disclosures such as financial results, share ownership, remuneration and related party transactions

(f) **The responsibility of the board** – guidance on the key functions of the board, including review of strategy, overseeing acquisitions and maintaining the integrity of the accounting and financial reporting systems.

3.2 IFAC identify what they believe to the key drivers of sustainable organisational success. By sustainable, they mean something that can be managed over the longer-term, not something that results in short-term success, to the detriment of long-term shareholder value.

(a) **Customer and shareholder focus** – understanding how to identify and satisfy end-user needs

(b) **Effective leadership and strategy** – providing ethical and strategic leadership in respect of value creation

(c) **Integrated governance, risk and control** – balancing performance and conformance in governance

(d) **Innovation and adaptability** – adapting the organisation to changing circumstances

(e) **Financial management** – implementing good practice in areas such as treasury, working capital and profitability improvement

(f) **People and talent management** – enabling people and talent management as a strategic function

(g) **Operational excellence** – supporting decision making with timely information

(h) **Effective and transparent communication** – engaging effectively with stakeholders

3.3 CIMA have added to the international debate by suggesting the following improvements to global governance codes.

(a) **Create a new reporting structure**

- Including more specific reports in governance in the chairman's statement

- Integrating the narrative of governance throughout the financial statements

(b) **Telling the governance story**

- Setting the tone from the top, starting with the chairman's statement

- Demonstrate how the board works as a team

- Linking the activities of the board to the key corporate events, using graphics if required to link actions to events

- Board effectiveness explained in terms of how performance is evaluated and how this links to remuneration

- Communication and engagement with stakeholders explained via detailed reporting on how the investor relations were managed

(c) **Compliance reporting**

- Demonstrate compliance via a tracker embedded within the chairman's statement

Activity 3: OECD principles

Required

Which of the following is part of the OECD principles of corporate governance?

A Creating integrated reporting structures
B Effective leadership and strategy
C Disclosure and transparency
D Compliance reporting

Solution

- Corporate governance is the system by which organisations are directed and controlled.

- Corporate governance problems can result from the agency problem and lack of shareholder activism.

- Key drivers for the development of corporate governance:

  - Increasing internationalisation and globalisation
  - Issues concerning financial reporting.

- The following symptoms can indicate poor corporate governance:

  - Domination by a single individual
  - Lack of involvement of board
  - Lack of adequate control function
  - Corporate greed
  - Lack of contact with shareholders.

- Corporate governance is usually regulated by voluntary codes, which interact with the law and the general ethical framework of society. Codes can be either principles based, or rules-based.

- The OECD provides the global benchmark for international corporate governance codes and encompass:

  - Ensuring the basis for an effective corporate governance framework

  - The rights and equitable treatment of shareholders and key ownership functions

  - Institutional investors, stock markets and other intermediaries

  - The role of stakeholders in corporate governance

  - Disclosure and transparency

  - The responsibility of the board.

- IFAC identify the following factors as being key to sustainable business success:

  - Customer and shareholder focus
  - Effective leadership and strategy
  - Integrated governance, risk and control
  - Innovation and adaptability
  - Financial management
  - People and talent management
  - Operational excellence
  - Effective and transparent communication.

- CIMA have identified the following improvements to corporate governance:
  - Creation of a new reporting structure
  - Telling the governance story
  - Compliance reporting.

- **Agency theory:** views the managers of an organisation as acting in an agency capacity, seeking to service their own self-interest, and looking after the performance of the company only to the extent where this promotes their own interests. This gives rise to the agency problem.

- **Corporate Governance:** is the system by which organisations are directed and controlled. Running an organisation of any type requires no specific qualifications, and there is no 'rule book', corporate governance aims to fill this gap.

- The **stakeholder theory** takes a more organic view of an organisation that goes beyond mere stewardship and states that the management has a duty of care not just to the owners, but also to the wider stakeholder community.

- **Stewardship theory:** views the management of an organisation as its stewards, tasked with managing its assets in line with the wishes of the owners.

Activity answers

Activity 1: Stakeholder theory

D   Stakeholder theory views companies as entities that owe a duty of care to the wider community. The other statements are incorrect as agency theory encourages directors to be selfish, stewardship theory views the directors as stewards, not stakeholders, and corporate governance empowers boards to erode the power of CEOs.

Activity 2: Corporate governance

Robert's actions are an example of strong management. ☐

Incorrect – Robert's actions are unethical and probably illegal.

Rupert was correct to carry out the instruction of the CEO. ☐

Incorrect – Rupert should have refused and if necessary reported this to the rest of the Board.

The governance within the company appears to be weak. ☐

Correct – Robert is a dominant influence and appears to be surrounded by weak executives.

Robert's actions are correct but unethical. ☐

Incorrect – Robert's actions cannot be justified.

Activity 3: OECD principles

C   Disclosure and transparency. Options A and D are part of CIMA's recommendations, whilst B is one of IFAC's drivers of sustainable corporate success.

1   Corporate governance is the system by which organisations are .... and
    ....

2   Which **two** of the following are symptoms of poor corporate governance?

    A   Lack of board involvement
    B   Bonuses for directors
    C   The finance director also performing the role of company secretary
    D   Inadequate supervision

3   The UK has taken a rules-based approach to corporate governance whereas the USA
    has taken a principles-based approach.

    True   ☐
    False   ☐

4   Which of the following is often cited as the main cause of corporate governance
    problems?

    A   Increasing profitability of listed companies
    B   The separation of ownership and control in companies
    C   'Fat cat' salaries of executive directors
    D   Lack of enforcement of the UK Corporate Governance Code

5   Who formulated the global benchmark for corporate governance codes?

    A   IFAC
    B   CIMA
    C   Sarbanes-Oxley
    D   OECD

Governance and corporations

5

Learning outcomes

Having studied this chapter you will be able to:

- Describe the role of the board and different board structures
- Explain the effects of corporate governance on directors' powers and duties
- Describe the types of policies and procedures that constitute 'best practice'
- Describe the respective committees and their roles and responsibilities with regards monitoring and controlling the actions of the Executive

Syllabus context

Each country has its own specific codes, ranging from the 'comply or explain' approaches of the UK Code and the King Report, to the rules-based Sarbanes-Oxley Act in the USA. In each instance, the codes aim to spell out best practice in order to ensure high standards of governance within listed companies. Whilst these codes are mandatory for listed entities, they may be voluntarily adopted by any organisation.

Chapter overview

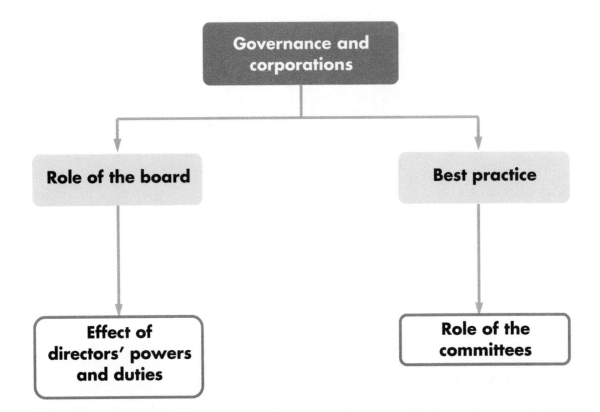

1 Role of the board

1.1 The board of a company is broadly responsible for taking **major policy and strategic decisions**. In order to discharge their responsibilities, the board should have an appropriate mix of skills and experience, and as we will see later, their performance should be regularly assessed.

1.2 The scope of the board's responsibilities are wide and include the following:

   (a)   Monitoring and even dismissing the chief executive
   (b)   Overseeing strategy
   (c)   Monitoring risks and control systems
   (d)   Monitoring human capital
   (e)   Ensuring effective communications with stakeholders
   (f)   Developing corporate social responsibilities and ensuring they are met.

1.3 The board of any company are expected to be:

   (a)   **Independent** – pursuing the company's interests above their own
   (b)   **Objective** – capable of rationale and bias-free decision making
   (c)   **Sceptical** – eager to question information provided to them
   (d)   **Resourceful** – capable of innovative leadership.

1.4 The **shareholders** of a listed company are commonly among its most important stakeholders. In these companies, the directors are tasked with running the company on their behalf as it is impractical to involve the shareholder body in the day-to-day running.

1.5 Shareholders only becomes involved in decision making at a very high level, by voting on resolutions at the AGM. Where shareholders become dissatisfied with the performance of the board, they can exercise their power by voting again on the re-election of the current executive team.

Illustration 1

In 2015 Anthony Jenkins, the CEO of Barclays plc, was ousted in a boardroom coup. The group's non-executive directors took behind-the-scenes steps through Sir Mike Rake, the most senior independent director, to remove Jenkins after a series of presentations in which the current strategy was discussed.

Rake, who orchestrated Jenkins' departure, said: "I reflected long and hard on the issue of group leadership and discussed this with each of the non-executive directors. Notwithstanding Antony's significant achievements, it became clear to all of us that a new set of skills were required for the period ahead. This does not take away from our appreciation of Antony's contribution at a critical time for the company."

Board structures

1.6 The UK model of corporate governance is based upon the idea of a **single**, or **unitary board**. The board is made up of a mix of executive and non-executive directors, all having the right to participate in board meetings. Best practice advises that half the board should be subject to annual re-election.

1.7 In European countries, a dual board structure is more common, consisting of:

Key term

Supervisory board	consisting of workers representatives and stakeholder management representatives. The board has no executive function, although it reviews the company's direction and strategy and is responsible for **safeguarding stakeholders' interests**.
Management board	composed entirely of managers, it is responsible for the day-to-day running of the business. The **supervisory board appoints the management board**, and membership of the two boards is mutually exclusive.

1.8 In Japan, the three tier board is commonplace:

(a) **Policy board** – setting long-term strategic issues

(b) **Functional boards** – made up of senior executives with functional roles

(c) **Monocratic boards** – fulfils more of a symbolic role with few real responsibilities.

Activity 1: Governance

Required

Corporate governance is **not** concerned with which of the following?

A   Business efficacy

B   Effective control

C   Fiduciary duties — law

D   Accountability

Solution

Impact of corporate governance

1.9 Company directors have always worked under duties imposed by a mix of **statutory duties** imposed by company law, as well as general **common law** duties, to exercise reasonable skill and care; and the **fiduciary duties** to not abuse the position of trust they occupy.

1.10 Corporate governance does not affect these duties, it merely adds additional duties on top of them, such as the need to engage constructively with shareholders, and to manage risk responsibly.

2 Best practice

2.1 The UK Corporate Governance Code (The 'Code') provides guidance on best practice. It operates on the basis that companies ought to '**comply or explain**'.

Key term

> **Comply or explain** means that should a company choose, or be unable to comply with the Code, then the instance(s) of non-compliance should be disclosed and explained in the financial statements to satisfy the requirements of the stock market listing rules.

2.2 In instances of non-compliance (such as in the Marks and Spencer illustration earlier) then it is up to the shareholders of the company to decide if they are satisfied with the explanation(s) for non-compliance. In this regard, the UK approach to corporate governance is regarded as voluntary.

2.3 The code has five main principles:

A   Leadership
B   Effectiveness
C   Accountability
D   Remuneration
E   Relations with shareholders.

2.4 **Leadership**

Effective leadership by the board has the following supporting principles:

A1. Board should be effective and accept **collective responsibility**

A2. A **division of responsibility** is required; no person to have unfettered powers

A3. **Chairman** to be responsible for **leading** the board

A4. Non-executive directors (NEDs) to **constructively challenge** and help develop strategy.

2.5 Effectiveness

Effectiveness has the following supporting principles:

B1. Board to have a balance of skill, experience, knowledge and independence

B2. A formal rigorous procedure for appointing directors

B3. Directors should commit sufficient time to the role

B4. Directors should refresh and develop their skills and knowledge

B5. Board should be supplied with quality information on a timely basis

B6. The board should rigorously appraise its own performance annually

B7. All directors to be subject to annual re-elections.

2.6 Accountability

Effective accountability by the board has the following supporting principles:

C1. Board should present a **balanced** and **understandable assessment** of the company's position

C2. Board should maintain **sound risk management** and **internal control** systems

C3. The **audit committee** should maintain an appropriate relationship with the company's auditors.

2.7 Remuneration

Effective remuneration by the board has the following supporting principles:

D1. **Executive directors' remuneration** should be designed to promote the long-term success of the company. Performance-related elements should be transparent, stretching and rigorously applied.

D2. No director should be involved in **setting** their **own pay.**

2.8 Relations with shareholders

Effective shareholder relations by the board has the following supporting principles:

E1. Board should maintain a **dialogue** with **shareholders**
E2. The **AGM** should be used to communicate with investors.

Activity 2: UK Code

Required

Which of the following statements are true?

The CEO is responsible for monitoring the performance of the chairman. ☐

Half the board should be subject to annual re-election. ☐

The Board should be effective and accept collective responsibility. ☐

Directors should benchmark their own pay to ensure fairness. ☐

Solution

2.9 The approaches of other countries varies, from the UK style approach of **South Africa's King Report**, to the ultra-prescriptive **Sarbanes-Oxley** regulations of the **USA**.

2.10 Owing to the voluntary compliance approach in the UK, corporate governance has had little direct **legal impact on company directors**. The Code is not a piece of statute, and contains no penal provisions.

3 Committees

3.1 Aside from attendance at board meetings, the way in which NEDs exert their control is by sitting on three committees.

Audit committee

3.2 The audit committee should consist of at least three, or for smaller companies, two, independent NEDs, at least one of whom has recent and relevant financial experience.

3.3 The committee should be chaired by an independent NEDs, who cannot also be the chairperson of the board.

3.4 Audit committees are responsible for:

(a) Appointing, compensating and overseeing the external auditors
(b) Monitoring the accounts
(c) Reviewing internal controls and risk management systems
(d) Considering the external auditors' independence and objectivity

(e) Approving any non-audit work awarded to the external auditors

(f) Reviewing the work of the internal auditors

(g) Reviewing whistleblowing procedures.

Appointments committee

3.5 This is sometimes referred to as the **nominations committee**. The majority of the nomination committee should be independent NEDs who are responsible for:

(a) Overseeing the process for making board appointments

(b) Making recommendations to the board on appointments

(c) Considering the balance between executive and independent NEDs

(d) The need for continuity and size of the board.

3.6 Any recommendations made by the appointments committee should be made on merit using objective criteria.

Illustration 2

James Murdoch's appointment as chairman of Sky plc in 2016 was publically criticised by some shareholders. Angry shareholders argued that Murdoch's appointment flouts the corporate governance code, and is a serious conflict of interest given he runs its biggest shareholder, Fox. For example Royal London Asset Management, which owed £50m of Sky shares, branded Murdoch's reappointment as "inappropriate".

Murdoch, a non-executive director at Sky, was the only candidate put forward by the company's nominations committee. Murdoch was then unanimously voted chairman by his 11 fellow board members, six of whom are independent directors.

A corporate governance manager at RLAM, said the process raised questions over how Murdoch was appointed. "His appointment is a major concern because the chairman should be independent. Particularly so in this case, as Fox is such a significant shareholder, even showing an interest in taking over Sky". It is surprising the board has chosen to elevate him to the level of chairman again."

The Guardian 2016

Remuneration committee

3.7 The remuneration committee plays a primary role in establishing remuneration arrangements. To be effective, the committee needs to determine the organisation's general remuneration policy as well as the specific remuneration packages for each director.

3.8 In order to ensure independence, the following controls are applied:

(a) All members are independent NEDs

(b) Member's connections with the company are examined for:

• Personal interest other than as shareholders

- Conflicts of interests
- Day-to-day involvement in running the business.

3.9 The recommendations of the remuneration committee are put to a non-binding shareholder vote at least every three years.

Illustration 3

In 2016 BP shareholders rejected a proposed pay package of almost £14m for chief executive Bob Dudley at the oil company's annual general meeting. Just over 59% of investors rejected Mr Dudley's 20% pay increase, one of the largest rejections of a corporate pay deal in the UK.

Such votes are non-binding but none-the-less the company chairman promised to review future pay terms. Mr Dudley received the rise despite BP's falling profits and job cuts as he had met the targets set within his service contract.

Activity 3: Committees

Required

1 According to the UK Corporate Governance Code, what two board committees should companies have?

A Nomination and remuneration.
B Audit and election.
C Remuneration and compliance.
D Nomination and risk.

Solution

Chapter summary

- The main source of corporate governance in the UK at this time is the UK Corporate Governance Code.

- Corporate governance rules have not changed directors' fiduciary and statutory duties, or their duties of skill and care under common law.

- The board should be responsible for taking major policy and strategic decisions and they are expected to be:

  - Independent
  - Sceptical
  - Objective
  - Resourceful.

- Best practice is laid out in the UK Code, under five main headings of:

  - Leadership
  - Effectiveness
  - Accountability
  - Remuneration
  - Relations with shareholders.

- The executive board is controlled by a balance of NEDs.

- NEDs will control key committees overseeing:

  - Audit
  - Appointments
  - Remuneration.

Keywords

- **Comply or explain:** means that should a company choose, or be unable to comply with the Code, then the instance(s) of non-compliance should be disclosed and explained in the financial statements to satisfy the requirements of the stock market listing rules.

- **Management board:** composed entirely of managers, it is responsible for the day-to-day running of the business. The supervisory board appoints the management board, and membership of the two boards is mutually exclusive.

- **Supervisory board:** consisting of workers representatives and stakeholder management representatives. The board has no executive function, although it reviews the company's direction and strategy and is responsible for safeguarding stakeholders' interests.

Activity 1: Governance

C The other options are correct, but fiduciary duties are imposed by and regulated by the law - not corporate governance.

Activity 2: UK Code

The CEO is responsible for monitoring the performance of the chairman – incorrect, it is the other way round.

Half the board should be subject to annual re-lection – incorrect, the whole board should be subject to annual re-lection.

The board should be effective and accept collective responsibility – correct.

Directors should benchmark their own pay to ensure fairness – incorrect, directors should not set their own pay.

Activity 3: Committees

A An organisation should set up a nomination committee to make recommendations on all new board appointments; and a remuneration committee, to review the pay of executive directors. It should also have an audit committee. In addition, it is recommended that an audit committee is set-up, though not having an audit committee can be justified on the grounds of size of the company and its lack of complexity.

Test your learning

1   What does the UK Corporate Governance Code recommend regarding the number of non-executive directors on the board?

   A   They should be the majority

   B   They should be the minority

   C   They are not required on the main board

   D   They should have enough of a presence so that power and information is not concentrated in one or two individuals

2   What does the UK Corporate Governance Code recommend regarding the roles of chairman and chief executive?

   A   The roles must be combined

   B   The chief executive should not go on to be chairman at a later date

   C   The chairman's role must be performed by a non-executive director, and the chief executive's, by an executive director

   D   Individuals selected for either role must hold a professional qualification

3   Audit committees are generally staffed by a company's auditors.

   True   ☐
   False ☐

4   Which of the following is not one of the elements of the UK Code of Corporate Governance?

   A   Effectiveness
   B   Leadership
   C   Compliance
   D   Remuneration

5   How does the UK Code Corporate operate?

   A   Comply or resign
   B   Honour and obey
   C   Explain or diverge
   D   Comply or explain

The role of audit

6

Learning outcomes

Having studied this chapter you will be able to:

- Identify the requirements for external audit and the basic processes undertaken
- Explain the meaning of fair presentation
- Distinguish between external and internal audit
- Explain the purpose and basic procedures of internal audit; the need for financial controls and the purpose of audit checks and audit trails
- Explain the role of internal audit in non-financial monitoring and control activities
- Illustrate the added value internal audit provides to both the board and the management of the corporation
- Explain the nature of errors
- Explain the nature of fraud
- Describe the different methods of fraud prevention and detection

Syllabus context

Audit is a form of assurance – giving the owners of an organisation some confidence in the accuracy of their organisation's financial statements. The external auditor's work will focus almost exclusively on whether the financial statements present a 'true and fair view' of the company's position. Internal auditors aim to add value to the company by looking at all aspects of its operations including, but not limited to, operational efficiency, IT systems, value for money and whether a company is meeting its corporate objectives. It is the responsibility of the internal auditors to detect fraud and errors.

Chapter overview

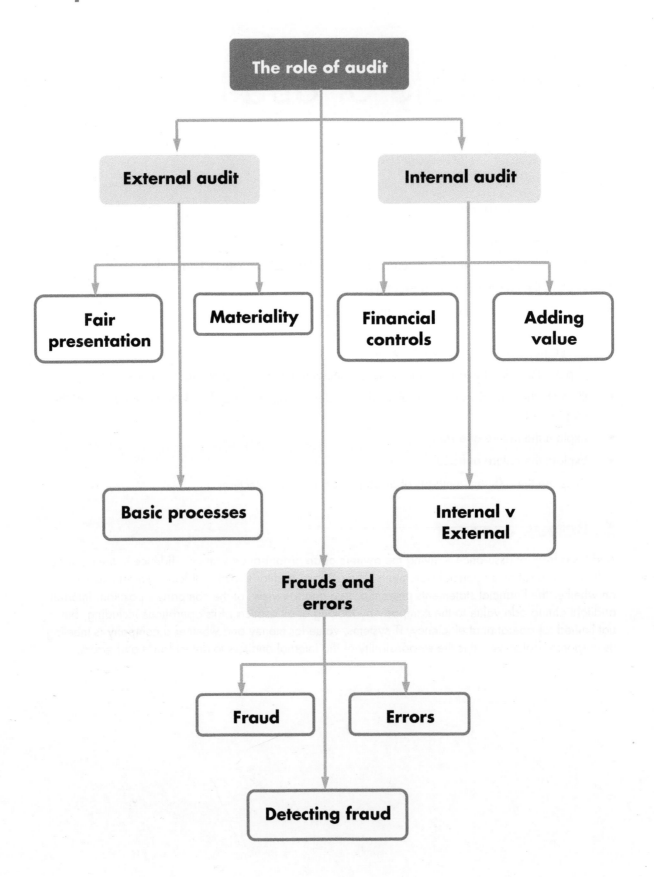

The role of audit

External audit

Internal audit

Fair presentation

Materiality

Financial controls

Adding value

Basic processes

Internal v External

Frauds and errors

Fraud

Errors

Detecting fraud

1 The nature of external audit

> An **external audit** is a type of **assurance engagement** that is carried out by an auditor to give an independent opinion of a set of financial statements.

1.1 All companies are required to be audited by statute, unless they are exempt by virtue of having satisfied two of the following requirements:

   (a) **Turnover** < £10.2m
   (b) **Total assets** < £5.1m
   (c) **Number of employees** < 50.

1.2 The objective of an audit of financial statements is to enable the auditor to **express an opinion** on whether the financial statements are prepared, in all material respects, in accordance with an applicable financial reporting framework.

1.3 The **purpose** of the external audit is to enable the auditors to give an opinion on the financial statements.

1.4 The audit opinion implies certain things to be true, amongst them:

   (a) **Adequate accounting records** have been kept.

   (b) The **accounts agree** with the accounting records and returns.

   (c) **All information and explanations** have been received which the auditor believes are necessary for the purposes of the audit.

   (d) Details of **directors' emoluments** and other benefits have been **correctly disclosed** in the financial statements.

> **Fair presentation**
>
> The auditors' report on the company's financial statements is expressed in terms of **truth and fairness**. This is generally taken to mean that the financial statements are:
>
> (a) Factual
> (b) Free from bias
> (c) Reflect the commercial substance of the business's transactions.

1.5 There are no legal definitions of true and fair, but they are taken to mean:

   (a) **True** – information is factual and conforms with reality. In addition, the information conforms with required standards and law. The financial statements have been correctly extracted from the books and records

   (b) **Fair** – information is free from discrimination and bias and in compliance with expected standards and rules. The accounts should reflect the commercial substance of the company's underlying transactions.

Materiality

1.6 Materiality is a key concept in auditing, as a material misstatement compromises the fair presentation of the financial statements.

1.7 Materiality is a somewhat subjective concept as is of often described as the level of error at which a reader's view of a set of financial statements changes. Whilst there is no statutory definition of material the following benchmarks are commonly used:

(a) 5% of profit before tax.
(b) ½ to 1% of gross profit.
(c) ½ to 1% of revenue.
(d) 1 to 2% of total assets.
(e) 2 to 5% of net assets.
(f) 5 to 10% of profit after tax.

Basic processes

1.8 A well-designed audit will encompass the following stages.

(a) An audit plan is created covering:
  - Engagement terms
  - Initial risk assessments
  - Timetable for work.

(b) An interim audit can be undertaken at which stage:
  - The company's systems of internal control are documented
  - **Tests of control** are undertaken
  - Limited **substantive testing** is undertaken.

(c) A final audit is performed, consisting of:
  - Substantive testing of the financial balances and statement of profit loss
  - Obtaining third party confirmations
  - **Analytical review** of the financial statements
  - A subsequent review
  - Agreeing the financial statements to the accounting records
  - Considering the going concern status.

Key term

| **Tests of control** | are audit procedures designed to evaluate the operating effectiveness of controls in preventing or detecting or correcting material misstatements. |

1.9 To gain assurance, the auditors will:

(a) Enquire and document the controls
(b) Re-perform transactions
(c) Inspect control mechanisms.

Key term

Substantive tests are those designed to detect material misstatements.

1.10 They include:

(a) Agreeing or reconciling the financial statements to the underlying accounting records

(b) Examining material journal entries

(c) Examining other adjustments made in preparing the financial statements.

Key term

Analytical review involves testing large volumes of predictable data by developing an expected balance, comparing to the actual data, and reconciling any material differences.

Illustration 1

David is the junior auditor working on the statutory final audit of Labyrinth Ltd and his review of last year's file and this year's interim audit have left him with concerns in three areas:

1 whether large purchases are being correctly classified as capital expenditure or revenue expenses

2 accounts receivable may be overstated

3 the wage and salary expense looks very high

For item 1, David could perform a test of control. He could raise a dummy large purchase and then check the ledgers to see if this has been correctly identified as a capital purchase and added to non-current assets.

For item 2, David could identify the 10 largest year-end debtors and write to those companies, asking them to confirm their year-end balance. By reconciling these responses to the client's ledger, he can substantively gain assurance over a material value of the accounts receivable balance.

For item 3, David could take last year's wages and salary expenses and adjust them forwards, taking account of changes in the company's average employee number and any centrally agreed wage rises. This will give an expected balance for the current year which he can compare to the actual figure. If any material differences remain, he can substantively investigate, following this analytical review.

Activity 1: External audit

Required

Which of the following statements is correct in relation to external statutory audits?

A   External audits give total assurance that the financial statements are free from all misstatement.

B   External audits give limited assurance that the financial statements are free from fraud and error.

C   External audits give complete assurance that the financial statements are true and fair.

D   External audits give reasonable assurance that the financial statements are free from material misstatement.

Solution

2 Internal audit

Key term

| **Internal audit** | is an independent appraisal function within an organisation designed to examine and evaluate its activities as a service to the organisation. The objective of internal auditing is to assist members of the organisation in the effective discharge of their responsibilities. To this end, internal auditing furnishes them with analyses, appraisals, recommendations, counsel and information concerning the activities reviewed. |

2.1   In the UK, the Turnbull Report, published in 1999 stated that listed companies who choose not to have an internal audit function should annually review the need to have one. Organisations with an internal audit function should annually review its **scope**, **authority** and **resources**.

2.2   The objectives of an internal audit function includes:

    (a)   Reviewing accounting and internal control systems

    (b)   Examining the financial and operating information

    (c)   Review of the economy, efficiency and effectiveness of operations

    (d)   Review of compliance

    (e)   Review of the safeguarding of assets

    (f)   Review the implementation of corporate objectives

(g) Identification of the significant business and financial risks, and monitoring the adequacy of the organisation's risk management policies

(h) Special investigations, as and when required.

Financial controls

Key term

> **Financial controls** are essential to ensure that an organisation is accurately recording its transactions.

2.3 Internal auditors will need to satisfy themselves that controls are in place to cover the following areas:

(a) **Revenue and cash collections** – recording orders, sales and receipts

(b) **Acquisitions and expenditures** – invoice processing, purchase orders

(c) **Production or conversion** – inventory movements

(d) **Financial capital and payment** – interest and dividend payments

(e) **Personnel and payroll** – joiners, leavers, salaries, bonuses

(f) **External financial reporting** – applying financial reporting policies.

2.5 To gain assurance over financial controls, the internal audit function will rely upon **audit checks** and **audit trails**.

2.6 Audit checks will include the same sorts of tests that external auditors deploy, a mix of test of control, substantive test and analytical review.

Adding value

2.7 Whilst the internal audit function is responsible for auditing the integrity of the financial controls, its scope extends far beyond this. Some specific examples of how and where audits can add value include:

(a) **Value for money audits** – how to improve the economy, efficiency and effectiveness of operations

(b) **IT audits** – assessing current capability and future flexibility of an organisation's IT systems

(c) **Operational audits** – assessing the effectiveness of management and processes

(d) **Procurement audits** – effectiveness of purchasing operations.

2.8 The outcome of any internal audit investigation should be a formal report to management, shared with the audit committee, and where appropriate, the external auditors. This report should take the form of:

(a) Terms of reference – defines the scope of the investigation
(b) An executive summary – high level summary
(c) Main body - outlining the purpose, scope and results of the audit
(d) Conclusions and recommendations – containing action points
(e) Appendices – supporting analysis.

Illustration 2

BABA Ltd operates a heavy manufacturing plant, and keen to improve its efficiency and reduce its environmental footprint, it tasks its internal auditors with finding ways of making the plant more energy efficient.

Bjorn is the senior internal auditor, and having spent 12 weeks reviewing the productive operations of the company, makes the following recommendations:

1   A Net Present Value calculation shows that if the company invests £2.5m in a new networks of pumps and pipes, hot water from the foundry can be used to replace the current central heating system. The investment will take six years to pay back and yield a positive NPV of £3.2m over the 20 year expected life of the equipment needed.

2   All light bulbs in the factory complex can be replaced with low energy bulbs and light sensors, saving the company £45,000 per year for an initial investment of £18,000.

3   Production staff efficiency could be improved by up to 8% if sickness, lateness and absenteeism were reduced. He recommends linking pay to performance by instituting a system where pay rises are limited to 1% plus half of any gains made in productivity, such that a gain of 6% of throughput would give staff a wage rise of 4% (1%+ 3%).

Activity 2: Efficiency

Required

Which of the following statements defines 'efficiency'?

A   The relationship between the goods and services produced and the resources needed to produce them.

B   Attaining the appropriate quantity and quality of physical, human and financial resources at the lowest cost.

C   The concern with how well an activity is achieving its policy objectives or other intended effects.

D   Determining the extent to which an organisation is managing its risks to a level acceptable to stakeholders.

Solution

External v Internal audit

	Internal audit	External audit
Responsible to	Management	Shareholders
Responsible for	Any task requested by management	Opinion on truth and fairness
Activities	Anything	Testing
Standards	Anything	Laws and regulations eg GAAP and IAS

3 Errors and fraud

Errors

3.1 There are three principle types of error that can affect financial record keeping:

(a) Errors of **omission** – either partial or total omission from the books of prime entry eg failing to record a sale

(b) Errors of **commission** – errors that arise during the recording or posting of a transaction that has been recorded eg recording a £10,000 sale as a £1,000 sale

(c) Errors of **principle** – recording a transaction in violation of accounting standards eg classifying a stationery order as a capital purchase.

Fraud

Key term

> **Fraud** has been legally defined as '**a false representation of fact, made with the knowledge of its falsity, or without belief in its truth, or recklessly careless, whether it be true or false**'.

3.2 Common frauds will include:

(a) **Ghost employees** – payments are collected for employees who don't exist

(b) **Collusion** with third parties – eg in the award of contracts

(c) **Inflating expense claims** – either individually or in collusion with other staff

(d) **Stealing assets** – either physically or virtually (eg online scams such as 'phishing')

(e) **Manipulation** of financial statements – either for personal or corporate gain.

3.3 For fraud to occur, the following conditions must be in place:

(a) **Dishonesty** – eg dishonest employees or contractors
(b) **Opportunity** – eg poor controls
(c) **Motive** – eg employees with grievances or financial problems.

Detecting fraud

3.4 An effective fraud prevention plan will include the following aspects:

(a) **Segregation of duties** to introduce supervisory controls
(b) **Documentation** to create audit trails
(c) **Prohibition** of certain activities such as sharing passwords
(d) **Limitation controls** such as approved supplier and authorisation limits
(e) **Internal audit investigations** of suspicious transactions/actions.

3.5 Aside from these general controls organisations will also rely upon:

(a) **Spot checks** – such as assets verification
(b) **Reconciliations** – such as cash and receivables accounts
(c) **Control accounts** – such as payroll, sales and purchases.

Illustration 3

In 2002, the internal audit department of US telecoms giant, WorldCom uncovered an $11bn accounting fraud that had been committed by its CEO, Bernie Ebbers.

This most astounding aspect of this fraud was its breath-taking simplicity. Over a period of many years Ebbers had orchestrated the capitalisation of almost every piece of mundane expenditure, including stationery items such as staplers and pens. This lead to a mass inflation of the company's net current assets as the profit or loss account was only recording the depreciation on these items, rather than their full cost.

Ebbers was sentenced to 25 years for this fraud of principle as well as conspiracy and filing false documentation as the company lost $180bn in value and was forced to shed over 30,000 jobs.

Activity 3: Errors

Raul was distracted by posts to his social media page whilst inputting some data into his company's accounting system. His lack of concentration resulted in him booking a sale against the account of Mr Bill, instead of Mr Ben.

Required

Which type of error has Raul committed?

A   An error of mistake

B   An error of omission

C   An error of commission

D   An error of principle

Solution

- An **external audit** is a type of assurance engagement that is carried out by an auditor to give an independent **opinion** on a set of financial statements.

- An audit provides **assurance** to the shareholders and other stakeholders of a company on the financial statements because it is independent and impartial.

- The auditor's report on company financial statements is expressed in terms of truth and fairness. This is generally taken to mean that financial statements:

- Are **factual**
- Are **free from bias**
- Reflect the **commercial substance** of the business's transactions.

- External audits give reasonable assurance that the financial statements are **free from material misstatement**.

- Most companies are required to have an audit by law, but some small companies are **exempt** based upon **turnover**, **net assets** and **employee numbers**.

- **Internal audit** assists management in achieving the entity's corporate objectives, particularly in establishing good corporate governance.

- Internal auditors are employed as part of an organisation's system of controls. Their responsibilities are determined by management and may be **wide-ranging**.

- Although many of the techniques internal and external auditors use may be similar, the basis and reasoning of their work is different.

- Internal audit has two key roles to play in relation to organisational risk management:

- Ensuring the company's risk management system operates effectively

- Ensuring that strategies implemented in respect of business risks operate effectively.

- Internal audit can be involved in **many different assignments** as directed by management. These can range from value for money projects to operational assignments looking at specific parts of the business.

- The internal auditors' **report may take any form**, as there are no formal reporting requirements for these reports as there are for the external auditor's report.

- Internal audit departments may consist of employees of the company, or may be outsourced to external service providers.

- **Errors** can be classified as **omissions**, **commission** or **principle**

- It is the **responsibility of management** and those charged with governance to **prevent and detect fraud**, and, in this respect, internal auditors may have a role to play.

- **Fraud prevention** relies on techniques such as segregation of duty, authorisation limits, supervision, documentation and prohibition.

Keywords

- **Analytical review:** involves testing large volumes of predictable data by developing an expected balance, comparing to the actual data, and reconciling any material differences.

- An **external audit** is a type of assurance engagement that is carried out by an auditor to give an independent opinion of a set of financial statements.

- **Fair presentation**

  The auditors' report on the company's financial statements is expressed in terms of truth and fairness. This is generally taken to mean that the financial statements are:

  (a) Factual
  (b) Free from bias
  (c) Reflect the commercial substance of the business's transactions.

- **Financial controls:** are essential to ensure that an organisation is accurately recording its transactions.

- **Fraud:** has been legally defined as 'a false representation of fact, made with the knowledge of its falsity, or without belief in its truth, or recklessly careless, whether it be true or false'.

- **Internal audit:** is an independent appraisal function within an organisation designed to examine and evaluate its activities as a service to the organisation. The objective of internal auditing is to assist members of the organisation in the effective discharge of their responsibilities. To this end, internal auditing furnishes them with analyses, appraisals, recommendations, counsel and information concerning the activities reviewed.

- **Substantive tests:** are those designed to detect material misstatements.

- **Tests of control:** are audit procedures designed to evaluate the operating effectiveness of controls in preventing or detecting or correcting material misstatements.

Activity 1: External audit

D   Statutory audits give reasonable assurance. It is not possible to give total or complete assurance, and is not focused on fraud.

Activity 2: Efficiency

A   Attaining the appropriate quantity and quality of physical, human and financial resources at the lowest cost. B describes Economy, C describes Effectiveness and D is about Risk Management.

Activity 3: Errors

C   Inputting a transaction is an error of commission - errors that arise during the recording or posting of a transaction that has been recorded.

Test your learning

1   Which of the following controls will help prevent fraud in an organisation? Tick all that apply.

   A   Obtaining references when recruiting
   B   Code of ethics
   C   Whistleblowing channels
   D   Segregation of duties

2   Which of the following will NOT be assessed in determining if a company is exempt from statutory audit?

   A   Number of employees
   B   Turnover
   C   Net current assets
   D   Net assets

3   'External auditors have no obligations to perform procedures or make enquires regarding the financial statements after they have been issued'.

   True   ☐
   False ☐

4   To ensure transparency the internal audit team should report to?

   A   The board of directors
   B   The audit committee
   C   The board of directors and the audit committee
   D   The shareholders

5   Corporate governance guidelines in the UK prohibit the purchase of internal audit services from external providers.

   True   ☐
   False ☐

Corporate social responsibility

7

Learning outcomes

Having studied this chapter you will be able to:

- Describe the OECD general policies
- Explain the role of national and international laws and regulations
- Describe the conflicting demands of stakeholders
- Describe the guidelines of reporting CSR within annual reports
- Identify synergies and tensions with CSR and brand management
- Identify issues with CSR and the supply chain

Syllabus context

The theme of social responsibility and sustainability focuses on the question of how far a business is accountable to the wider community for the effects of its operations. Opinions vary from viewing a company as part of society, and therefore being duty bound to be a responsible citizen, to the view that they exist solely to maximise the wealth of investors, and it being the job of governments to create a fair society. Arguments in recent years lean towards the former view, and this is reflected in the increasing trend for companies to seek sustainable working practices; those which allow the company to trade profitably whilst minimising their environmental footprint.

Companies that pursue positive CSR policies often reap brand benefits. However, in doing so, they must be careful to stay true to those policies; else they risk being exposed as 'greenwashing' eg merely paying lip service to CSR and sustainability in a cynical attempt to win favour with consumer markets.

Chapter overview

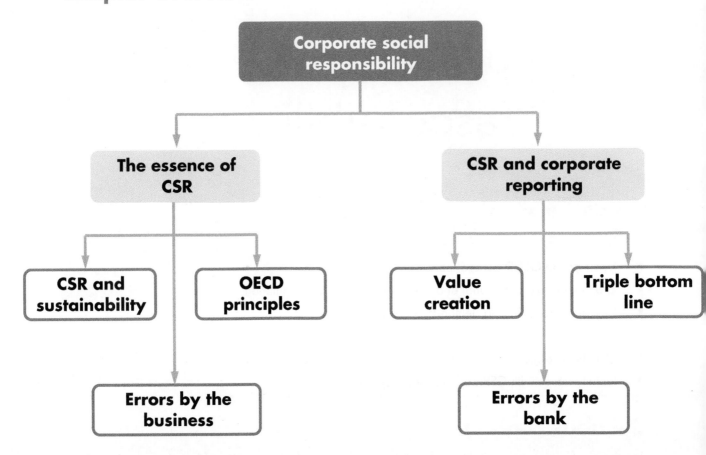

1 The essence of Corporate Social Responsibility (CSR)

> **CSR** is an organisation's obligation to maximise positive stakeholder benefits while minimising the negative effects of its actions.

Key term

CSR and sustainability

> **Sustainability** Central to this is the concept of sustainability; developing strategies so that the company only uses resources at a rate that allows them to be replenished, such that the needs of the current generation can be met without compromising the needs of future generations.

Key term

1.1 Importantly, CSR includes **economic and legal issues**, as well as ethical ones: reflecting the whole range of stakeholders who have an interest in an organisation. In this respect, CSR requires an organisation to go beyond simply adhering to minimum ethical standards. Ethics concerns issues such as justice, fairness and honesty, which are fundamental, unchanging values that have implications for business.

1.2 CSR is more closely associated with contemporary business issues, and concerns organisations giving something back to society, and being good citizens. Therefore, in contrast to ethics, CSR is socially mediated and likely to be specific to the time and culture in which it is considered. For example, CSR could include:

(a) Equal opportunity policies.
(b) Policies on environmental emissions.
(c) Policies on fair trade.
(d) Charitable donations.
(e) Policies on standards in the supply chain.

OECD principles

1.3 The OECD has issued extensive guidance to multinational companies on how they should develop policies that take into account countries in which they operate and the views of other stakeholders. Their general policies are:

1 Contribute to economic, social and environmental progress with a view to **achieving sustainable development**.

2 **Respect the human rights** of those affected by their activities consistent with the host government's international obligations and commitments.

3 **Encourage local capacity building** through close co-operation with the local community, including business interests, as well as developing the enterprise's activities in domestic and foreign markets, consistent with the need for sound commercial practice.

4 **Encourage human capital formation**, in particular by creating employment opportunities and facilitating training opportunities for employees.

5 **Refrain from seeking or accepting exemptions** not contemplated in the statutory or regulatory framework related to environmental, health, safety, labour, taxation, financial incentives, or other issues.

6 Support and uphold **good corporate governance principles** and develop and **apply good corporate governance practices**.

7 Develop and apply **effective self-regulatory practices** and management systems that foster a relationship of confidence and mutual trust between enterprises and the societies in which they operate.

8 **Promote employee awareness** of, and compliance with, company policies through appropriate dissemination of these policies, including through training programmes.

9 **Refrain from discriminatory or disciplinary action** against employees who make *bona fide* reports to management or, as appropriate, to the competent public authorities, on practices that contravene the law, the guidelines or the enterprise's policies.

10 Encourage, where **practicable, business partners**, including **suppliers** and **sub-contractors**, to apply principles of corporate conduct compatible with the guidelines.

11 Abstain from any **improper involvement in local political activities**.

1.4 Whilst much an of organisation's CSR policies could be viewed as voluntary commitments; in reality, these are often shadowed by associated legal or regulatory obligations. For example:

(a) **Equal opportunity policies** – these are often demanded by employment legislation.

(b) **Policies on environmental emissions** – national governments often set targets on CO2 emissions, backed up by 'green taxes' or carbon levies.

(c) **Policies on fair trade** – low pay can be tackled by minimum wage legislation.

(d) **Charitable donations** – usually attract generous tax reliefs.

(e) **Policies on standards in the supply chain** – commonly regulated by minimum wage and health and safety regulations.

Illustration 1

The Kyoto Protocol is an international agreement linked to the United Nations Framework Convention on Climate Change, which commits its parties by setting internationally binding emission reduction targets.

Recognising that developed countries are principally responsible for the current high levels of GHG emissions in the atmosphere as a result of more than 150 years of industrial activity, the protocol places a heavier burden on developed nations under the principle of "common but differentiated responsibilities."

The Kyoto Protocol was adopted in Kyoto, Japan, on 11 December 1997 and entered into force on 16 February 2005. The detailed rules for the implementation of the Protocol were adopted at COP 7 in Marrakesh, Morocco, in 2001, and are referred to as the "Marrakesh Accords". Its first commitment period started in 2008 and ended in 2012.

The British retailer Marks and Spencer plc has a high profile CSR campaign entitled 'Plan A'. Between 2007 and 2015, the company claimed its enhanced CSR policies had the following impacts:

Customers – 2.8bn carrier bags saved

Products – 32% of cotton used in clothing comes from more sustainable sources

Suppliers – 32% of M&S Food comes from suppliers that meet the M&S Silver sustainability standard

Operations – Zero, M&S is the world's only major retailer with carbon neutral operations

Employees – 5,000 paid volunteering days in 2014/15

Shareholders – £160m net benefit generated by Plan A in 2014/15.

Plan A Report 2015 Marks and Spencer.

CSR conflicts

1.5 There are arguments both in favour and against CSR, given that it involves companies going above and beyond their legal obligations.

1.6 The arguments in favour of CSR include:

(a) **Customer expectations** eg fair trade coffee is now the norm

(b) **Brand name** – can help differentiate a company name

(c) **Lower environmental costs** – less waste attracts less disposal costs

(d) **Staff benefits** – can help attract / retain quality employees

(e) **Funding opportunities** – some investors look specifically for ethical investments

(f) **Avoidance of punitive legislation** – voluntary standards can negate the need for laws

1.7 The arguments against investment in CSR include:

(a) **Businesses do not have responsibilities** – only people have responsibilities, they should shoulder the burden

(b) **Shareholders rule** – the aim of a company is solely to maximise shareholder wealth, they can spend their dividends on charity if they want

(c) **Governments regulate society** – social fairness is the job of governments, not companies

(d) **Diversion of focus** – companies should focus on their businesses, not solving society's ills.

1.8 The most common source of conflict will therefore be between shareholders and the other stakeholders in a company. These may include:

(a) **Shareholders** – typically looking for long-term financial returns via dividends and capital growth

(b) **Debt investors** – expecting interest payments and return of capital

(c) **Employees** – want job security, fair remuneration and training, and development opportunities

(d) **Suppliers** – looking for continuity of supply at profitable prices

(e) **Customers** – generally have choice and information, and typically looking for best value for money

(f) **Governments** – require legal compliance with positive benefits of employment and tax receipts

(g) **Regulators** – demand compliance backed with threat of fines

(h) **Local communities** – want responsible employer who takes care of the local environment.

1.9 As each of these stakeholders have different objectives, and varying degrees of power and interest, **conflicts will be inevitable** eg whilst a company wants to maximise profits for shareholders, it will want to minimise the prices it pays to suppliers; maximise the prices it charges customers, keep wage inflation as low as possible whilst minimising the rates at which it pays taxes.

CSR and the supply chain

1.10 Of particular relevance is the impact of CSR on the supply chain of a business. If an organisation claims to adopt sustainable practices, then it follows that these commitments must extend through the supply chain. This has the following consequences:

(a) **Standards** – suppliers must meet the organisation's own standards.

(b) **Audit** – supplier's adherence to standards must be verified.

(c) **Reputation** – CSR failures in the supply chain will reflect on the organisations' own reputation and brands.

(d) **Prices** – higher prices may be payable to uphold CSR commitments.

Activity 1: CSR and mission statements

Large companies often include a reference to social responsibility in their mission statements.

Which of the aspirations below reflect a genuine concern for socially responsible behaviour?

(i) To support the local community and preserve the environment
(ii) To keep employees informed of policy, progress and problems
(iii) To pay all employees the minimum wage or higher

A (i) and (ii)
B (i) and (iii)
C (ii) and (iii)
D (i), (ii) and (iii)

Solution

2 CSR and corporate reporting

2.1 The integration of CSR commitments and progress within an organisation's financial statements has become increasingly common in recent years. Traditional corporate reporting, which focuses on financial performance, is said to only tell part of the story.

2.2 Integrated reporting is concerned with conveying a wider message on an entity's performance. It is not solely centred on profit, or the organisation's financial position, but details how its activities interact to create value over the short, medium and long term.

2.3 The **International Integrated Reporting Council** identified seven guiding principles which support the preparation of an integrated report:

(a) **Strategic focus and future orientation** – how strategy will create value over the short, medium and long term

(b) **Connectivity of information** – detailing how capitals (see below) are being used to achieve strategic goals

(c) **Stakeholder relationships** – how key stakeholder groups are managed

(d) **Materiality** – disclosure of matters which are likely to impact upon the ability to create value

(e) **Conciseness** – giving users the information they require, and no more

(f) **Reliability and completeness** – information should be free from material error and bias

(g) **Consistency and comparability** – consistent use of KPIs year-on-year.

Value creation

2.4 In 2013, the International Integrated Reporting Council (IIRC) introduced the integrated reporting framework. The framework refers to an organisation's resources as 'capitals'.

2.5 Capitals are used to **assess value creation**. Increases or decreases in these capitals indicate the level of value created or lost over a period. Capitals cover various types of resources found in a standard organisation. Integrated reporting refers to **six different types of capital**.

2.6 The integrated reporting framework classifies the capitals as:

(a) **Financial capital** – the pool of investment funds available covering equity, debt and grants

(b) **Manufactured capital** – the infrastructure available to help the organisation deliver goods and services

(c) **Intellectual capital** – intangible assets such as patents and licences

(d) **Human capital** – the experience and capability of the workforce

(e) **Social and relationship capital** – the relationships and networks that an organisation has cultivated

(f) **Natural capital** – available environmental resources such as minerals.

Triple bottom line

2.7 An alternative approach is advocated by John Elkington, chairman of the think-tank SustainAbility Ltd. He writes about the triple bottom line (TBL), which means 'business people must increasingly recognise that the challenge now is to help deliver simultaneously':

(a) **Economic prosperity** – the economic benefit enjoyed by the host society. It is the lasting economic impact the organisation has on its economic environment. Importantly, however, this is not as narrow as the internal profit made by a company or organisation

(b) **Environmental quality** – a TBL company endeavours to benefit the natural order as much as possible, or at the least do no harm and curtail environmental impact eg the company tries to reduce its ecological footprint

(c) **Social justice** – fair and beneficial business practices towards labour and the community and the region in which a corporation conducts its business.

2.8 Elkington's TBL is sometimes summarised as **Profit, Planet** and **People**.

Illustration 2

CIMA itself is taking a lead in integrated reporting. Within its financial statements KPIs are published in the following areas, in addition to the statutory sections such as the Statement of Profit or Loss and Statement of Financial Position:

Value chain – number of new students acquired

Resources and relationships – employability of CGMA members

Value creation – operating surplus

Notable examples of companies that have adopted the TBL approach are:

- SAS
- Google
- NetApp
- Zappos.com
- Dreamworks Animation

CSR and branding

2.9 A positive CSR strategy can have brand benefits, as increasing number of consumers are sensitive to issues such as the sustainability of the goods and services that they buy.

2.10 In order to maximise the brand benefits of investments in CSR, three alternative approaches are available:

(a) **Integrated approach** – the brand and CSR operate in synchrony. This is appropriate where CSR is a key driver of brand preference eg organic food producers

(b) **Selective approach** – CSR is developed in certain and specific ways, for example via the use of sub-brands and strategic partnerships eg Unilever acquiring Ben and Jerry's

(c) **Invisible approach** – CSR plays an important and philosophical role in guiding a company, but is understated in external communications and initiatives. This allows companies to use CSR as an asset to bolster trust in their brand and company. Fashion giant, Hennes & Mauritz (H&M) is an example. Whilst they have deeply embedded CSR policies in all aspects, they do not flaunt these.

2.11 It is clear that positive CSR policies can have brand benefits, and these can transfer into positive financial benefits too. There does, however, remain a risk that poor CSR can cause tremendous brand damage too.

Illustration 3

In 2010, BP suffered its first annual loss for nearly 20 years, following the catastrophic explosion at the Deepwater Horizon oil rig in the Gulf of Mexico which cost it at least £25 billion. Some analysts think the total cost to shareholders could exceed £40 billion over the next ten years from 2010–2020.

2010 was one of the most damaging year's in BP's history as the devastating explosion, which killed 11 workers and triggered the biggest offshore oil spill in history, shattered the company's reputation.

In February 2011, BP's chief executive said he was determined to see BP 'emerge from this episode as a company that is safer, stronger, more sustainable, more trusted and also more valuable...2011 will be a year of recovery and consolidation as we implement the changes we have identified to reduce operational risk and meet our commitments arising from the spill. But it will also be a year in which we have the opportunity to reset the company, adjusting the shape of our business, and focus on growing value for shareholders.'

Investors claimed that BP executives and directors breached their fiduciary duties to the company by ignoring safety and maintenance for years before the well exploded on 20 April 2010. The investors' lawyers argued that, despite warnings about the safety of the well, BP continued to systematically cut budgets.

Investors (who had filed a claim against BP claiming diminished share value) claimed that in addition to the tragic loss of life which resulted from the blowout, the disaster is anticipated to cost the company billions of dollars in damages, permanent reputational harm and intense government scrutiny. The claimants argued that, despite existing concerns raised by federal safety regulators, BP had cut operational costs by 15% in 2009 alone (the year before the disaster). In their opinion, 'This reduction in budgets and manpower further undermined the company's ability to operate safely, as personnel were stretched even thinner, and resources that should have been devoted to maintenance, monitoring and addressing crucial safety failures in every aspect of the company's operations were diverted.'

Bloomberg 2011

Activity 2: Six capitals

The International Integrated Reporting Council identifies the capitals used to created value. Which of the following is NOT one of the six capitals?

A   Financial
B   Intellectual
C   Natural
D   People   (Human Capital)

Solution

Chapter summary

- **CSR** is an organisation's obligation to maximise positive stakeholder benefits while minimising the negative effects of its actions. Within this, **sustainability** refers to the ability to trade without depleting the earth's resources.

- CSR typically sees a company **voluntarily going above and beyond its legal minimum** requirements, through activities such as charitable giving and treatment of staff.

- The **OECD** has issued extensive guidance to multinational companies on how they should develop policies that take into account countries in which they operate and the views of other stakeholders, highlighting 11 areas of general guidance.

- CSR can be **controversial** as some view the policies pursued as being the **responsibilities of other** entities such as governments, citizens and charities.

- Companies are increasingly integrating CSR reporting into their financial statements. The **International Integrated Reporting Council** identifies seven guiding principles which support the preparation of an integrated report.

- The **six capitals** used to measure value creation identified by the IIRC are:

  - Financial capital
  - Manufactured capital
  - Intellectual capital
  - Human capital
  - Social and relationship capital
  - Natural capital.

- The **Triple Bottom Line** approach identifies three ways of measuring sustainable success:

  - Economic prosperity   (Profit)
  - Environment quality   (Planet)
  - Social equity   (People).

- Good CSR policies can have brand benefits, the differing approaches to seeking synergies in this area are:

  - **Integrated** approach
  - **Selective** approach
  - **Invisible** approach.

Keywords

- **CSR:** is an organisation's obligation to maximise positive stakeholder benefits while minimising the negative effects of its actions.

- **Sustainability:** Central to this is the concept of sustainability; developing strategies so that the company only uses resources at a rate that allows them to be replenished, such that the needs of the current generation can be met without compromising the needs of future generations.

Activity 1: CSR and mission statements

A   (i) and (ii)

Social responsibility relates to an organisation's obligation to maximise positive stakeholder benefits while minimising the negative effects of its actions. It reflects the whole range of stakeholders who have an interest in an organisation.

However, social responsibility entails more than simply conforming with legislation, which is what option (iii) is describing. By paying a minimum wage to its employees, an organisation would be fulfilling its legal obligations, not its social responsibilities.

Activity 2: Six capitals

D   People is incorrect, this is part of the triple bottom line approach. The six capitals refers to Human Capital rather than People.

Test your learning

1   Which of the following statements about Integrated Reporting are true:

(i)   An integrated report should provide an insight into an organisation's ability to create value in the short, medium and long term.

(ii)   An integrated report should provide an insight into how an organisation recognises and responds to the interests of its stakeholders.

(iii)   The primary focus of an integrated report is an organisation's financial performance.

A   (i) and (ii) only
B   (i) and (iii) only
C   (ii) and (iii) only
D   (i), (ii) and (iii)

2   Which of the following are elements of the IIRC's seven guiding principles which support the preparation of an integrated report? Select all that apply.

A   Reliability and completeness
B   Truth and fairness
C   Materiality
D   Shareholder relations   (– Stakeholder Rels....)

3   CSR and ethics are similar concepts, but CSR is only part of ethics which is a much wider area.

True   ☐
False   ☑   ethics – subs w/n CSR

4   Beta plc is a multinational food producer. In 2012, they took the leading step to only use organic and fair-trade produce in its products. These practices feature heavily in Beta's corporate mission statement and are prominent in the company's advertising.

Which of the following approaches to CSR and branding is Beta taking?

A   Integrated
B   Implied
C   Selective
D   Invisible

5   Good CSR policies (will) — may increase the value of an organisation's brand.

True   ☐
False   ☑

Contract formation 1

8

Learning outcome

Having studied this chapter you will be able to:

- Identify the essential elements of a valid simple contract, and situations where the law requires the contract to be in a particular form

- Explain how the law determines whether negotiating parties have reached agreement

Syllabus Context

The vast majority of contracts can be formed with little or no formality eg buying a newspaper from a shop. However, there are certain contracts that are required to either be in writing, or, be evidenced in writing. An example of this that you are probably familiar with is the need to exchange and complete written contracts when buying a house.

Chapter overview

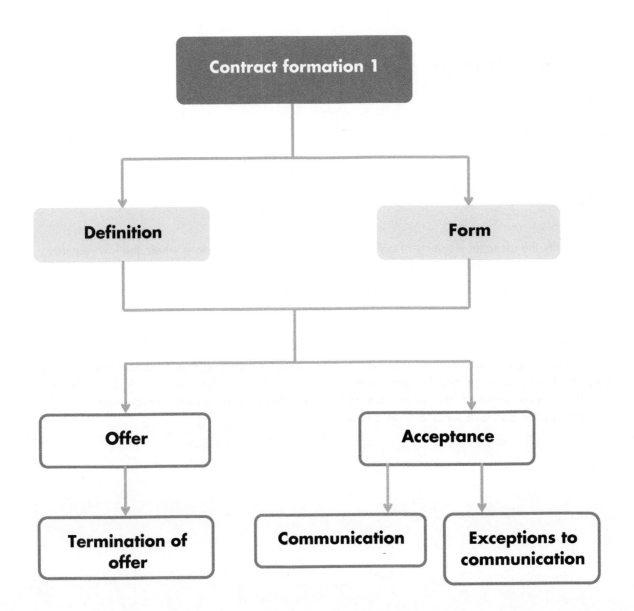

1 Contract basics

The **contract** may be defined as an agreement which **legally binds** the parties, or an agreement which the law will **recognise** and **enforce**.

1.1 Some key definitions to be aware of include:

Agreement is made by offer and acceptance

Consideration both parties must bring something of value to the contract

Intention the parties must have an intention to create legal relations between themselves.

Vitiating factors are those that can render a contract void, including the following:

(a) **Form**: some contracts must be made in a particular form

(b) **Terms**: must be properly incorporated into the contract

(c) **Consent**: a misrepresentation made by one party may affect the validity of the contract

(d) **Legality**: the courts will not enforce a contract which is deemed to be illegal or contrary to public policy

(e) **Capacity**: certain bodies can only make contracts within the boundaries of their authority; also, generally people lack contractual capacity if they are under the age of 18.

1.2 An invalid contract may be:

Void there is no contract

Voidable the innocent party can withdraw from the contract

Unenforceable the contract is valid but performance by one party cannot be enforced.

Illustration 1

Bobby wishes to sell his car, and knows that his nephew, Junior, is due to sit his driving test soon and is looking for a reliable motor. Bobby's car has a full service history and Junior, who has just turned 17, agrees to pay £500 for the car in a week's time. When Junior's parents, Cliff and Sue-Helen, hear about this, they are upset as they had already bought Junior a car as a surprise present, so they insist that the contract with Bobby is cancelled.

In this instance, the advice is quite straightforward, as Junior is only 17, so he does not have the capacity to enter into a contract with Bobby. As Junior lacks contractual capacity, the contract is unenforceable, so Bobby cannot sue him, or, insist on Junior complete the contract as agreed.

2 The form of a contract

2.1 **General rule,** a contract may be made in **any form**. It may be **written**, or **oral**, or **inferred** from the conduct of the parties. However, a number of **commercial contracts** must be made **in writing** or in **a particular form**.

Illustration 2

A customer in a self-service shop may take his selected goods to the cash desk, pay for them and walk out without saying a word.

2.2 The following contracts **must be in writing** for them to be legally enforceable:

    (a)   The transfer of shares in a limited company
    (b)   The sale or disposition of an interest in land
    (c)   Bills of exchange and cheques
    (d)   Consumer credit contracts
    (e)   Assignment of debts.

2.3 Certain contracts may be made orally, but are not enforceable in a court of law, unless there is written evidence of their terms. The most important contract of this type is the contract of **guarantee**.

2.4 Certain transactions must be exercised by **deed**:

    (a)   These must be in **writing** and must be **signed**

    (b)   **Delivery** must take place, consisting of conduct indicating that a person executing the deed intends to be bound by it.

2.5 The following contracts must be by deed. These are referred to as **speciality contracts**:

   (a)   **Leases** of three years or more

   (b)   The conveyance or transfer of a **legal estate** in land, including a mortgage

   (c)   A **promise** not supported by consideration (such as a covenant).

Activity 1: Deeds

Required

Which of the following contracts must be in the form of a deed?

A   Sale of shares
B   Consumer credit agreements
C   Sale of an interest in land
D   A covenant

Solution

3 Offer

Key term   An **offer** can be defined as '**an offer to be bound on specific terms, it must be certain**'.

3.1 By definition then, offers cannot be vague, imprecise, or open to interpretation. The person making the offer is known as the **offeror**, and person in receipt of an offer is known as the **offeree**.

Key term   It is essential that offers are distinguished from **Invitations to Treat** (ITT). This is merely something that acts as an **inducement** to encourage another person to make an offer, and is therefore not capable of acceptance itself.

3.2 Case law has defined the following as ITTs.

   (a)   Goods displayed in a shop window – *Fisher v Bell* **(1)**
   (b)   Goods on a shop shelf – *Pharmaceutical Society of GB v Boots* **(2)**
   (c)   Public advertisements – *Partridge v Crittenden* **(3)**
   (d)   A share prospectus
   (e)   An invitation to submit a tender

3.3 However, it is not always abundantly clear in the case of **public advertisements** as to whether or not the wording of such an advertisement has resulted in an offer being made, rather than an ITT, per *Carlill v Carbolic Smoke Ball Co (4)*. In this case, the pleas of the defence, amongst which were that their newspaper advert was merely an ITT, were undermined by the following facts.

(a) The **wording was too precise** to be deemed an ITT

(b) The advert was **addressed to the world at large**, not Mrs Carlill, hence worldwide offers are possible

(c) '**Money on the table**' signalled intention

(d) **Unilateral acceptance** was possible by Mrs Carlill, waiving the need for her to communicate her acceptance of the offer.

Illustration 3

Sanjay attends an auction, and when the bidding gets underway, he raises his hand to indicate he is prepared to pay £5,000 more than the previous bidder.

In this instance, any notices advertising the auction, and any accompanying catalogues/brochures would be classified as ITTs. When Sanjay raises his hand, he is bidding and therefore making legally binding offers to purchase the lot for sale.

Activity 2: Bobby's car

Bobby still needs to sell his car. He places a prominent notice in the window of his car reading "Car for sale, excellent motor, full service history. Will sell for offers in excess of £500".

How would you describe the legal effect of this notice?

A   It is an offer
B   It is a tender invitation
C   It is an invitation to treat
D   It is a deed

Solution

4 Termination of an offer

4.1 An offer is only capable of being accepted while it is deemed to be open. The following actions will result in the termination of an offer:

(a) **Express rejection** – saying no

(b) **Counter offer** – *Hyde v Wrench* **(5)**

- Although this should not be confused with a mere request for information as per *Stevenson v McLean* **(6)**

(c) **Lapse of time** either:

- Express
- Implied – *Ramsgate Hotel v Montefiore* **(7)**
- Or death of the offeror.

(d) **Revocation** subject to the following.

- It must be communicated at any time before acceptance – *Routledge v Grant* **(8)**

- It must actually be received by the offeree – *Byrne v Van Tienhoven* **(9)**

- Its communication may be via a reliable third party – *Dickinson v Dodds* **(10)**

- A promise to keep an offer open by the offeror is only effective when this promise has been bought by the offeree.

(e) **Failure of a condition** where an offer has terms and conditions attached that are not met.

(f) **Death of the offeree**, similarly as a general rule the death of the offeror terminates the offer also.

Illustration 4

Captain Jack makes an offer of £100,000 to purchase a used Schooner from Sparrow Marine Merchants, subject to the ship being 'seaworthy'. When Jack arrives to sail the ship away he notices a large hole in the hull, fractionally above the water line which had not been disclosed by the sellers.

In this instance there is a condition of the contract that the vessel will be 'seaworthy'. The damage to the hull would render this condition not satisfied and so Jack's offer to purchase the ship would be terminated.

5 Acceptance

Key term

Acceptance can be defined as 'the unconditional assent to all of the terms of the offer', as per *Neale v Merrett* **(11)**.

5.1 Once a valid offer has been accepted the parties are deemed to be '**in agreement**'.

5.2 Furthermore, acceptance must be made while an offer is open, and may only be made by an authorised person.

5.3 Where two parties enter into a protracted sequence of offer and counter offer, it is important to establish who offered last, and who accepted as per *Butler Machine Tools Co Ltd v Ex-Cell-O Corp* **(12)**.

Illustration 5

Whilst on holiday, John saw a rug he liked, being sold by Bjorn from his market stall. The price tag read £500, but John offered £300, which Bjorn refused. John offered £350, but Bjorn insisted he would not sell for less than £500. After John made a final offer of £450, which Bjorn rejected, John decided to look elsewhere for an alternative rug.

In this case, Bjorn's price tag is an ITT, and John proceeds to make three offers, all of which are rejected by Bjorn. We therefore have three offers, but no acceptance and hence, no contract of sale.

6 Communication of acceptance

6.1 The general rule is that **acceptance must be communicated** to the offeror, subject to the following rules.

    (a) Acceptance may be in the form of express words, either oral or written, or deeds – *Brogden v Metropolitan Railway Co* **(13)**

    (b) Acceptance may not be via silence –

Illustration 6: Case of Felthouse v Bindley

Mr Felthouse wanted to buy one of his nephew's horses. Felthouse wrote to his nephew who wanted to sell the horse to him, stating that "If I hear no more about him, I will consider the horse mine..." Subsequently, there was no notice from his nephew and Felthouse considered the horse to be his own.

The court ruled that Felthouse did not have ownership of the horse, as there was no communication of acceptance of the contract.

7 Exceptions to the communications rule

7.1 The need to communicate acceptance may be waived in the following circumstances:

(a) Where **unilateral acceptance** is possible – *Carlill v Carbolic Smoke Ball Co* **(4)**

(b) When the **postal rules** apply acceptance is completed as soon as the letter has been posted, subject to the following restrictions –*Adams v Lindsell* **(14)**:

(i) Letter must be properly addressed and stamped

(ii) Acceptance by post must be in the contemplation of both parties

(iii) The postal rules have not been excluded, this can be done with express or implied wording – *Holwell Securities v Hughes* **(15)**.

(c) Telegrams may also be subject to the postal rule – *Byrne v Van Tienhoven* **(9)**.

7.2 If the offeror mandates a specified method of communication, other equally speedy methods will suffice – *Yates v Pullen* **(16)**.

7.3 Instantaneous methods of communication are **not** subject to the postal rules, with acceptance being deemed to occur where and when communication is accepted – *Entores v Miles Far Eastern Corp* **(17)**.

received

Illustration 7

Dumblefield runs a prestigious tennis tournament and reserves 10% of its centre court tickets for sale each day on a 'first come, first serve' basis. Some tennis fans are so keen to ensure they get these tickets they sleep outside the complex in tents to ensure they are at the front of the queue each day.

In this instance Dumblefield have offered a set number of tickets with specific conditions attached so could be held to be making an offer. The actions of fans who camp can be interpreted as an attempt to accept this offer (unilateral acceptance), precluding Dumblefield from withdrawing the tickets from sale.

Activity 3: D and E

On 1 May, D wrote to E offering to sell him a quantity of cloth. On 14 May, E wrote to D, accepting this offer. Though D had not, in his letter to E, indicated that he required E to accept within any particular time, having received an offer from X to buy the cloth on 13 May, he had assumed that E did not intend to accept the offer to him (E) and accordingly, he sent a telegram to E, revoking it. It chanced that E's letter was posted and D's telegram sent at exactly 3 pm on 14 May.

Required

(a) Explain the general requirement for communication of acceptance.

(b) Why is the postal rule said to be an exception to that general rule?

(c) What are the requirements for the postal rule to apply?

  (i)
  (ii)
  (iii)

(d) Does the postal rule apply here? (Answer yes or no.)

(e) What is the rule on communication of revocation?

(f) In the scenario, who 'communicated' first, D or E?

(g) What other arguments could be put forward by D to avoid the contract?

(h) Is D likely to be successful if he puts forward the argument in (g) above?

Solution

Chapter summary

- A valid contract is a **legally binding** agreement, formed by the mutual consent of two parties.

- The law seeks to protect the idea of 'freedom of contract', although contractual terms may be **regulated by statute**, particularly where the parties are of unequal bargaining strength.

- Although most contracts may be made in any form, some must be made in a **particular form**. A number of commercial contracts must be **made in writing**, for example.

- The first essential element of a binding contract is **agreement**. This is usually evidenced by **offer** and **acceptance**. An offer is a definite promise to be bound on specific terms, and must be distinguished from the mere supply of information and from an **invitation to treat**. Acceptance must be unqualified agreement to all the terms of the offer. A **counter-offer** is a rejection of the original offer.

- Acceptance is generally **not effective until communicated** to the offeror, the principal exception being where the **'postal rule'** applies; in which case, acceptance is complete and effective as soon as notice of it is posted.

- The postal rule states that, where the use of the post is within the co**ntemplation of both the parties**, acceptance is complete and effective as soon as a letter is posted. This is even though it may be delayed or even lost altogether in the post.

- **Acceptance** can be defined as 'the unconditional assent to all of the terms of the offer', as per *Neale v Merrett* **(11)**.

- **Agreement:** is made by offer and acceptance

- **Consideration:** both parties must bring something of value to the contract

- The **contract** may be defined as an agreement which legally binds the parties, or an agreement which the law will recognise and enforce.

- **Intention:** the parties must have an intention to create legal relations between themselves.

- It is essential that offers are distinguished from **Invitations to Treat** (ITT). This is merely something that acts as an inducement to encourage another person to make an offer, and is therefore not capable of acceptance itself.

- An **offer** can be defined as 'an offer to be bound on specific terms, it must be certain'.

- **Unenforceable:** the contract is valid but performance by one party cannot be enforced.

- **Vitiating factors**: are those that can render a contract void, including the following:

  (a) Form: some contracts must be made in a particular form

  (b) Terms: must be properly incorporated into the contract

  (c) Consent: a misrepresentation made by one party may affect the validity of the contract

  (d) Legality: the courts will not enforce a contract which is deemed to be illegal or contrary to public policy

  (e) Capacity: certain bodies can only make contracts within the boundaries of their authority; also, generally people lack contractual capacity if they are under the age of 18.

- **Void:** there is no contract

- **Voidable:** the innocent party can withdraw from the contract

Activity answers

Activity 1: Deeds

D   Covenants must be in deed form. They should be in writing, signed by both parties and delivered.

Activity 2: Bobby's car

C   It is an invitation to treat as the notice is designed to promote interest in the car, which will then prompt interested parties to ring the owner and make an offer above £500. The word 'offer' is not conclusive, the courts will look at the substance of the statement rather than its form eg this is clearly an inducement rather than a statement which is clear and definite.

Activity 3: D and E

(a)   To be valid an acceptance must be actually communicated ie received.

(b)   This is because we can have acceptance without actual receipt ie deemed communication at posting.

(c)   (i)   Letter must be properly addressed and stamped.
      (ii)   Put into the post, and the post is in the contemplation of both parties
      (iii) Postal rule must not have been excluded.

(d)   Yes.

(e)   To be valid, communication of revocation must always be received.

(f)   E.

(g)   D could argue that his offer had lapsed through passage of time at the time that E sought to accept D's offer.

(h)   No. As there was no express time period specified, the offer would automatically lapse after a reasonable period – *Ramsgate Hotel v Montefiore*.

      What is reasonable depends upon the facts of each case. As cloth is neither price volatile nor perishable, the offer is unlikely to have lapsed within a two-week period.

1 A valid contract is a legally binding agreement. The three essential elements of a contract are (1) ...., (2) .... and (3) ....

2 A conveyance must be evidenced by deed.

   True ☐

   False ☐

3 Which one of the following is **NOT** a means by which an offer is terminated?

   A The period over which the offer is expressed to be kept open expires without acceptance by the offeree

   B The offeror tells the offeree before the latter's acceptance that the offer is withdrawn

   C The offer is accepted by the offeree

   D The offeree responds to the offer by requesting further information

4 **Fill in the blanks** in the statements below, using the words in the box.

   As a general rule, acceptance must be (1) .... to the (2) .... and is not effective until this has been done.

   An (3) .... is a definite promise to be bound on specific terms, and must be distinguished from a supply of (4) .... and from an (5) ....

   A counter-offer counts as (6) .... of the original offer

information	offer	invitation to treat
rejection	communicated	offeror

5 As a general rule, silence cannot constitute acceptance.

   True ☐

   False ☐

6 If two offers, identical in terms, cross in the post:

   A Either party may accept, to form a contract
   B The postal rule applies
   C The first offer to arrive is the basis for the contract
   D There is no contract as there is no acceptance

Case summaries

1 Fisher v Bell

Flick knife exhibited in shop window. Prosecuted for offering an offensive weapon for sale. It was held that display of an item in a shop window is an invitation to treat.

2 Pharmaceutical Society of Great Britain v Boots Cash Chemists

Held that the display of drugs on open shelves was merely an inducement to the buyer to make an offer to buy, not an offer to sell capable of acceptance.

3 Partridge v Crittenden

P placed ad regarding rare birds. RSPCA brought a court action for offering birds for sale. It was held that the ad was an invitation to treat and not an offer for sale.

4 Carlill v Carbolic Smoke Ball Co.

The Carbolic Smoke Ball Co advertised their product during an influenza epidemic as being able to stave off the flu. If anybody used their smoke ball in accordance with the printed instructions and caught the flu they would pay the individual £100. To show their good faith they deposited a sum of money with their bank.

Mrs Carlill caught flu after having used the product very carefully and claimed her £100. The company refuse to pay, saying that their advert was an invitation to treat only.

The Court held that this was in fact an offer to the whole world, the deposit of money showed intention to be legally bound and consideration was provided by the act of the customer using the product as instructed.

5 Hyde v Wrench

An offer to sell at £1,000 was met with a counter offer at £950. This was rejected. The subsequent acceptance at the original price was legally ineffective as that offer had been terminated by the counter offer.

6 Stevenson v Mclean

M offered to sell iron 'at £2.00 net cash per ton till Monday'.

Monday: S telegraphed to ask if M would accept £2.00 for delivery over 2 months or, if not, longest limit M would give.

10.01: M receives telegram.

1.34pm: S accepts by telegram.

M had sold to someone else. Advised S by telegram sent at 1.25pm which arrived at 1.46pm.

Court held S's first telegram was a request for information not a counter offer which did not terminate the original offer. A valid contract existed.

7 Ramsgate Victoria Hotel v Montefiore

M applied to buy shares in June. In November the company accepted his offer and requested balance. M said offer had expired. It was held that the offer was for a reasonable time only. Five months was much more than reasonable and so the offer had lapsed.

8 Routledge v Grant

G offered to buy horse requiring acceptance in 6 weeks. Within the 6 weeks he withdrew his offer.

It was held G could revoke his offer within the 6-week period as it was prior to acceptance. There was no consideration given by R to keep the offer open.

9 Byrne v Van Tienhoven

1 October	offer letter posted in Cardiff
8 October	revocation letter posted in Cardiff
11 October	offer letter received in New York. Telegram of acceptance sent.
15 October	letter confirming acceptance posted in New York
20 October	revocation letter received in New York

Held: the letter of revocation could not take effect until actually communicated on 20 October. There was a binding contract.

10 Dickinson v Dodds

10/6 complainant offered property for sale– offer to be open for 2 days

11/6 property sold to another buyer

A reliable 3rd party informed complainant of the sale

Complainant then accepted the offer

It was held that the defendant was free to revoke offer and had done so.

Complainant could not therefore accept the offer.

11 Neale v Merrett

An offer to sell land at £280 was accepted at the full price, enclosing £80 and an undertaking to pay the balance by instalment. This conditional acceptance of the offer had terminated it so no legal contract existed.

12 Butler Machine Tools Co Ltd v Ex-Cell-O Corp

On May 23, 1969, Butler Machine Tool offered to sell a machine tool to Ex-Cell-O. As part of the written offer the offeror was given precedence over any terms in the buyer's order. In reply to the offer Ex-Cell-O made an order for the machine on different terms. At the bottom of the order was written that that they accepted the order "on the Terms and Conditions stated". Butler replied, writing that the order was to be delivered "in accordance with our revised quotation".

Ex-Cell-O experienced some delay and could not accept the machine tool on time. Butler invoked the price increase clause for the period after which they had agreed the machine would be delivered. Ex-Cell-O refused to pay the extra charge and so Butler sued for breach of contract. Ex-Cell-O argued that the price increase clause was not part of the agreement. At trial the judge found in favour of Butler.

However on appeal Lord Denning held in favour of Ex-Cell-O. He found that the multiple letters should be read as a whole and single document. Following the ruling of Lord Cairns in the Brogden v Metropolitan case he stated that 'it will be found that in most cases when there is a "battle of forms" there is a contract as soon as the last of the forms is sent and received without objection being taken to it'. Therefore, judgment was entered for the buyers.

13 Brogden v Metropolitan Railway Co

Brogden was a colliery owner in Wales. From early 1870 he supplied the Metropolitan Railway Company (Railway) with coal and coke, in varying quantities and at varying prices. In November 1871 a representative of Brogden suggested that a contact should be entered into. Representatives of each side met and prepared a draft agreement that referred to quantities, quality, price and other matters. The draft was prepared by the representative of Railway, who handed it to the representative of Brogden for approval. The head of the firm filled in some parts, altered some words, filled in the arbitration clause by nominating an arbitrator, appended the word "Approved" and signed it in his own name and not the firm name, but did not date the document. The document was returned to Railway, the expectation being that a more formal document would be prepared in duplicate for execution. This never happened, but on 22 December 1871 Railway placed an order in terms of the document, which Brogden fulfilled. The parties traded thereafter on the terms of the document until December 1873, when Brogden declined to continue to supply on that basis. Railway brought action for breach of contract by Brogden.

In his summary Lord Cairns decreed:

Brogden had supplied coal to Railway. On 18 April 1871 it wrote indicating that prices were rising, but that it would be prepared to make a contract for a year's supply, at a fixed price. The parties met on 19 December 1871, and Railway handed over a contract form, with blanks. Brogden returned the draft on 21 December 1871 with some additions, alterations, and the name of the arbitrator filled in. The parties were clearly headed for contract. It would be very strange if, having got to this point, nothing further was done. In fact, more was done. Railway commenced placing orders in terms of the contract, and Brogden commenced to fulfill orders and charge accordingly, maintaining the fixed price and agreed add-ons. Correspondence refers to a "contract", and the whole attitude is that both are bound to performance. Thus there was consensus.

14 Adams v Lindsell

L Made an offer requiring acceptance in 'course of post'

A accepted the offer 'in course of post' on 5/9

L received the reply on 9/9 but had already sold the goods

It was held that the acceptance was effective when posted.

15 Holwell Securities v Hughes

H gave HS an option to buy premises to be exercised 'by notice in writing'. HS sent a letter which was not received by H.

Held that there was no contract as 'notice' meant the letter must actually be received.

16 Yates Building Co v Pulleyn

Offer called for acceptance by registered delivery letter. Offeree sent ordinary letter which arrived without delay.

It was held that no disadvantage had been suffered and as such the offer was valid.

17 Entores Ltd v Miles Far East Corporation

E Ltd, in London, send offer to MFE, in Amsterdam, by teleprinter. Acceptance sent by MFE in Amsterdam by teleprinter to E Ltd in London.

MFE later in breach and question arose as to where contract was made and where litigation should begin.

Held that contract was made where acceptance actually communicated to E Ltd, therefore in London.

Contract formation 2

9

Learning outcomes

Having studied this chapter you will be able to:

- Explain how the law determines whether negotiating parties have reached agreement and the role of consideration in making that agreement enforceable

- Explain when the parties will be regarded as intending the agreement to be legally binding and how an agreement may be avoided because of misrepresentations

Syllabus context

Consideration is a sometimes complex concept; however at its heart, it is fundamentally simple. In order to form an enforceable contract, both parties must agree to exchange items of any value that they deem acceptable. Should either party wish to subsequently change the deal, then this must be agreed by both, as you cannot force the other person to agree to accept less, or to give more than was originally agreed.

In everyday life, intention is clear to see in most circumstances. In the exam, however, questions are likely to focus on situations where any expressions of intention are missing. Here you are going to have to follow the presumptions rooted in case law **BUT** remember these presumptions can always be rebutted with evidence to the contrary. Misrepresentations are covered separately in a later chapter.

Chapter overview

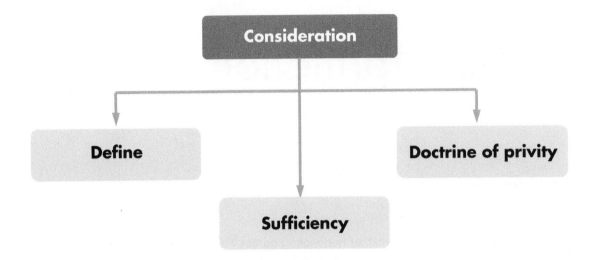

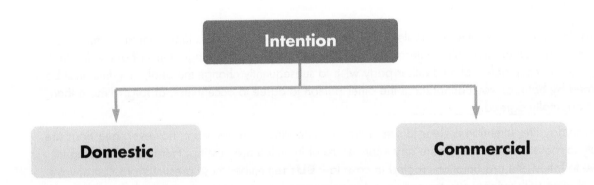

1 Definition of consideration

Key term

Consideration can be defined as '**the element of value in an agreement**', and in English law, must be supplied by both parties in order to form a binding contract.

1.1 Consideration can be in the form of money, goods, services, or the promise of any of these.

1.2 There are three forms of consideration.

(a) **Executory** – the promise to perform an action. Hence, contracts can be formed by an exchange of promises, known as an executory contract.

(b) **Executed** – an act given in return for a promise, the promise only becoming enforceable upon execution of the act.

(c) **Past** – the strict order is that consideration must be supplied after agreement has been formed. In cases where consideration is given before agreement, this consideration is deemed to be 'past' and not valid per *Re McArdle (1)*.

Note. Past consideration may be deemed valid where it can be proved there was an earlier implied promise to pay as per *Stewart v Casey (2).*

1.3 If there is an existing contract, and one party makes a further promise, no additional contractual obligations will arise. Even where such a promise is directly related to the previous bargain, it will be held to have been made upon past consideration.

Illustration 1

Brutus agreed to sell a puppy to his friend Olive for £200. Once negotiations were completed, Brutus assured Olive that the puppy was 'a pleasant dog, and suitable for a family home'. When Olive took the puppy home, it barked aggressively at her daughter and scratched her with his paws.

In this instance, the assurances about the puppy's temperament were made after the contract was formed, and as it was unsupported by fresh consideration, it does not fall within the original contract and Olive has no claim.

2 Sufficiency of consideration

2.1 In addition to the requirement that consideration not be in the past, the following general rules also apply,

(a) Performance must be **legal**, the courts will not enforce an illegal agreement

(b) Performance must be **possible**

BPP
LEARNING MEDIA

(c) Consideration must **'be sufficient but need not be adequate'** – *Thomas v Thomas (3)* and *Chappell v Nestlé (4)*, meaning that as long as there is **some element of value** in the deal, the courts are unlikely to intervene on behalf of a party who has signed a bad bargain.

2.2 Given that consideration needs to be sufficient, the courts have defined this term in two contexts.

(a) **Performance of existing contractual obligations** is not sufficient to support a promise of additional reward.

- For example, if the members of a large project team are promised an additional £100 each by their employer to complete a project in time to meet an existing deadline, where **one** of the team falls ill, they will not be able to enforce that promise as they are not providing additional consideration – *Stilk v Myrick (5)*

- However, should the £100 have been offered to them due to the illness of a **majority** of the project team members, then the promise is enforceable – *Hartley v Ponsonby (6)*

- The exception to the rule in *Stilk v Myrick (5)* is that where both parties derive a mutual benefit, then such a promise is enforceable – *Williams v Roffey Bros (7)*

(b) **To support a waiver of legal rights, where part payment is given in full settlement of a debt**, this part payment is not sufficient to support the promise to write off the unpaid debt as per *Pinnel's Case (8)*.

- For example, if you owed a friend £100, but could only repay £80, despite your friend's promise to never ask for the other £20, they could in fact demand this amount, as you have not provided any consideration to support this waiver of the debt.

- In order to support this waiver, additional consideration could be supplied in the following ways, subject to the agreement of the creditor:
  - pay the debt early
  - provide payment in kind
  - pay at a different location
  - payment is made by a third party.

2.3 A final exception to the rule in **Pinnel's Case** was revived by Lord Denning in his ruling on the **Equitable Doctrine of Promissory Estoppel** as per *Central London Property Trust v High Trees* **(9)**. In such instances where the following circumstances prevail, the creditor can be estopped from breaking their promise to waive a debt under the application of this equitable law:

- The creditor makes a promise to waive a debt
- The debtor relies upon that promise to their detriment
- The creditor is aware of the reliance made by the debtor.

2.4 Performance of a **statutory duty** is no consideration as per *Collins v Godefroy* **(10)**, unless the act performed amounted to additional services as per *Glasbrook Bros v Glamorgan CC* **(11)**.

Illustration 2

Roman, a wealthy mineral trader, decided to set up a professional football league in his own country, and founded one of the newly formed clubs, Diamond Lights FC, in his home town. Roman is dismayed to learn that the local police intend to charge him 2 million dramas to police each home game, to be played at 3pm on Saturday afternoons. Roman believes that policing the streets around the stadium falls within the police's statutory duties and is refusing to pay.

In this case, the football club would need to pay. The courts would find that the football club had voluntarily decided to hold matches on Saturday afternoons when large attendances were likely, thus increasing the risk of disorder.

Activity 1: Consideration

Which of the following statements are true of valid consideration?

need not be adequate but must be suff

  F ✗ (i)   Must be of adequate and sufficient value
  ✓ (ii) Must move from the promisee
  T ✓ (iii) Must be given in every binding agreement
  F ✗ (iv) May be given before a promise in return — *part consid*

- (A) (ii) and (iii) only
- B (iii) and (iv) only
- C (i), (ii) and (iii) only
- D (ii), (iii) and (iv) only

Solution

Saleem contracted with Mira to supply 50 handcrafted pots for £5,000. Saleem finished the order on time but Mira was unable to pay the full £5,000. She offered Saleem £4,000 in full and final settlement. Saleem reluctantly agreed. Saleem has now heard that Mira sold the pots to a retailer for £15,000. He now wants to receive the £1,000 shortfall.

Required

Advise Saleem.

Solution

3 Doctrine of privity

Key term

It is a general rule that only a party who is **privy** to a contract may enforce or sue on that contract, as per *Dunlop v Selfridge (12)*.

3.1 However, there are a number of common law and statutory exceptions to this rule:

(a) Where a collateral contract exists

(b) Where a contract has been validly assigned

(c) Where a contract has been created expressly for the benefit of a third party

(d) Motor insurance claims per the Road Traffic Act 1988

(e) The Contracts (Rights of Third Parties) Act 1999 whereby the third party has rights provided that:

- they are expressly identified in the contract
- the contract confers a benefit on them.

Activity 3: Bungle's paint

Rod commissioned Freddie to build a treehouse in his garden for his daughter Jane. Rod had a friend, Bungle, who was a specialist paint supplier, and Rod inserted a clause into his contract with Freddie that he was to buy some environmentally friendly paint from Bungle.

Unfortunately, the paint supplied by Bungle was faulty and the treehouse had to be repainted at a cost of £400 to Rod.

R + F
for Jane

Required

Which of the following statements is true?

- ✗ A   Jane can sue Bungle
- ✗ B   Rod cannot sue Bungle as they are friends
- ✓ C   Freddie cannot sue Bungle as he was merely acting under instruction from Rod   *he could.*
- Ⓓ   Rod can sue Bungle directly

Solution

R + F
by Jane.

---

4 Intention to create legal relations

4.1   In the absence of express written or verbal consent, the courts will make the following presumptions; however, it is important to note that any of these can be rebutted.

(a)   **Domestic and social arrangements**

- **Spouses living together** – No intention presumed – *Balfour v Balfour (13)*

- **Spouses separating** – Intention presumed – *Merritt v Merritt (14)*

- **Other friendly agreements** – No intention presumed, unless 'mutuality of intention' can be proved per *Simpkins v Pays (15)*

(b) **Commercial agreements**

- There is a very strong presumption of intent in such agreements as per *Edwards v Skyways* **(16)**

- However, even this can be rebutted, for example, in transactions deemed to be **binding in honour only** – *Jones v Vernons Pools* **(17)**

Activity 4: Peggy and Phil

Peggy runs a pub, and asked her son Phil to fix her car for her as he runs a garage. When Phil fixes the car, Peggy is shocked to receive a bill for £280 covering parts and labour. Peggy does not believe it is right for her son to charge her for a favour, and bars him from her pub.

Required

Which of the following statements are true?

F ☐ A mother and son can never enter into contractual relations

T ☐ Phil runs a business, so is acting in the course of commerce

F ☐ It is likely that Peggy will have to pay Phil, but for parts only

T ☐ Peggy is likely to be liable for the full amount

F ☐ As Peggy and Phil are not spouses, there cannot be a contract

☐ Peggy is liable under the 'mutuality of obligation' principle

Solution

Chapter summary

- Consideration is what each party brings to a contract. It is usually a **promise** in return for an **act** or **another promise**.

- Consideration need not be **adequate**, but it must be **sufficient**. This means that what is tendered as consideration must be capable in law of being regarded as consideration, but need not necessarily be equal in value to the consideration received in return.

- The principle of **promissory estoppel** was developed in *Central London Property Trust v High Trees House*. It means that in some cases, where someone has made a promise, they can be prevented from denying it.

- As a general rule, only a person who is a party to a contract has enforceable rights or obligations under it. This is the doctrine of **privity of contract**, as demonstrated in *Dunlop v Selfridge*.

- Both parties to a contract must **intend** the agreement to give rise to legal obligations. Their intentions may be express – 'this agreement is not subject to legal jurisdiction' – or may be inferred from the circumstances. **Social, domestic and family** arrangements are not assumed to be legally binding, unless the contrary is clearly shown. **Commercial** agreements are assumed to be legally binding unless the contrary is clearly demonstrated.

Keywords

- **Consideration:** can be defined as 'the element of value in an agreement', and in English law, must be supplied by both parties in order to form a binding contract.

- It is a general rule that only a party who is **privy** to a contract may enforce or sue on that contract, as per *Dunlop v Selfridge* **(12)**.

Activity answers

Activity 1: Consideration

A   Consideration need not be adequate. If it is given before a promise in return then it is invalid past.

Activity 2: Saleem's pots

To be binding, consideration must be sufficient. A promise to part pay a debt is insufficient consideration to support a waiver of contractual entitlement as per *Pinnel's case*. Exceptions have developed to this rule. These exceptions are derived both from common law and equity. The common law exceptions include payment at earlier date, payment in hand and payment by a third party. The equitable exception is promissory estoppel. On the facts of this case, none of the exceptions appear to apply; consequently, Saleem should be entitled to sue for the £1,000.

Activity 3: Bungle's paint

D   Rod can sue Bungle directly. When Rod instructed Freddie, he created a collateral contract which allows him to overreach the rule of privity. Jane is not privy to the contract, so cannot sue. Rod and Bungle's friendship is irrelevant to the situation, as this agreement is clearly of a commercial nature and thus, intention will be found. Freddie could sue Bungle, though this would only happen if Rod sued Freddie first, as Freddie would want to recover his losses from Bungle.

Activity 4: Peggy and Phil

Although Peggy and Phil are related it is very likely that the courts will find that this transaction was commercial in nature, and thus Phil will be able to enforce payment against his mother. The correct options are therefore:

- Phil runs a business so is acting in the course of commerce
- Peggy is likely to be liable for the full amount

1   Past consideration, as a general rule, is not sufficient to make a promise binding.

    True ☐
    False ☐

2   Consideration need not be (1) .... but it must be (2) ....

3   The rebuttable presumptions the courts will make with regard to parties' intention to create legal relations are: Social, domestic and family arrangements are generally intended to be binding. Commercial agreements are not generally intended to be binding.

    True ☐
    False ☐

4   Where an agreement is (1) .... in nature, the courts will strongly presume legal intention. However, when an agreement is (2) .... in nature, the courts will generally presume there is no intention.

5   Which of the following are valid exceptions to the rule that part-payment of a debt is not sufficient to discharge a debt in full.

    Payment in kind   ☐
    Payment at a deferred date   ☐
    Payment by a third person   ☐
    Payment via a collateral contract ☐
    Payment at the agreed location   ☐
    Payment via executory consideration ☐

Case summaries

1 Re McArdle

Decorating was done in the family home by a daughter-in-law and on the subsequent death of the mother-in-law, the remainder of the family promised to pay the cost of the decorating to the daughter-in-law when the estate was settled. This promise was not enforceable as the consideration to 'buy' the promise was provided in the past.

2 Stewart v Casey

The claimant was asked by the defendant to promote their patent. Once the work was finished, the defendant promised to pay the claimant. It was held that promotion work is normally paid for and this was implied at the outset. A valid contract therefore existed.

3 Thomas v Thomas

The executors of a man's will promised to let his widow live in his house, in return for a rent of £1 per year. It was held that £1 was sufficient consideration to validate the contract, although it did not represent adequate rent in economic terms.

4 Chappell v Nestle

Chocolate bar wrappers provided in exchange for a record offered by Nestle were part of the consideration despite having little or no commercial value. It was not cash alone which entitled the person to the record.

5 Stilk v Myrick

Two deserters on a sea voyage led to a promise from the captain to the crew to divide the deserters' wages between them if they sailed the ship home. It was held that the promise to pay extra was unenforceable as their contract already obliged them to meet normal emergencies and no additional consideration was provided.

6 Hartley v Ponsonby

More money was promised to sailors if they sailed the ship home when the level of deserters rendered the ship unseaworthy. This promise was enforceable as the sailors provided additional consideration by going beyond their obligation.

7 Williams v Roffey Bros and Nicholls (Contractors) Ltd

Roffey Bros were main contractors in the refurbishment of a block of flats. In the contract between Roffey Bros and the employer, there was a penalty clause which provided that Roffey Bros would have to pay damages if the work was not completed on time.

Roffey Bros had sub-contracted the carpentry work to Williams and became concerned that Williams would not be able to finish on time. Roffey Bros therefore offered Williams an extra £10,300 to finish the work on time. They later refused to pay the money when Williams completed on time.

It was held where that there was no evidence of fraud or economic duress and so there was a benefit to both parties, a promise backed up by consideration may be enforceable. Hence Roffey Bros were ordered to pay the £10,300.

8 Pinnel's Case

Cole owed Pinnel £8 10s, but at Pinnel's request, paid £5 2s 6d one month before the full sum was due. Cole claimed that there was an agreement that the part-payment would discharge the full debt. The court found in favour of Pinnel, because part-payment of an original debt did not make for fresh consideration. Therefore, the agreement was not a contract.

9 Central London Property Trust v High Trees House

During the war, CLPT made a promise not to increase the rent they charged HT. As a result, HT reduced the rent they charged their tenants. After the war Lord Denning hypothesised on what he would do if CLPT attempted to claim back the rent from HT on the basis that they had, in effect, received something (reduced rent) in exchange for nothing in return.

It was held that even though HT had given no consideration to CLPT for the promise, CLPT would be estopped from going back on the promise. They had entered into the promise freely with the intention that HT relied on it, and HT had done so, to their detriment (they passed on the rent reduction in full to their tenants).

10 Collins v Godefroy

The facts: The claimant had been subpoenaed to give evidence on behalf of the defendant in another case. He alleged that the defendant promised to pay him for appearing.

Decision: There was no consideration for this promise.

11 Glasbrook Bros v Glamorgan CC

The facts: At a time of industrial unrest, colliery owners, rejecting the view of the police that a mobile force was enough, agreed to pay for a special guard on the mine. Later they repudiated liability, saying that the police had done no more than perform their public duty of maintaining order, and that no consideration was given.

Decision: The police had done more than perform their general duties. The extra services given, beyond what the police in their discretion deemed necessary, were consideration for the promise to pay.

12 Dunlop v Selfridge

D imposed a resale price on customers when selling tyres to a dealer. The dealer sold tyres on to Selfridge with the same price restriction. S sold tyres at below price. D sued S

It was held that D could not recover damages under a contract to which it was not privy.

13 Balfour v Balfour

An informal maintenance agreement between husband and wife (who had not broken up) was held not to be legally binding.

14 Merritt v Merritt

A husband and wife separated. The husband agreed to pay the wife £40 per month, out of which she agreed to keep up the mortgage payments. The husband signed a note to this effect and in addition, agreed to transfer the house to his wife once the mortgage had been paid. On the discharge of the mortgage, the husband refused to effect a transfer.

The court held that all the circumstances of the case gave rise to an inference of legal intention and hence, the agreement was legally binding.

15 Simpkins v Pays

Agreement to share competition winnings can be enforceable if there is 'mutuality in the arrangements between the parties'.

16 Edwards v Skyways

In commercial arrangements, there is a presumption of intention to create legal relations which will have to be discharged by the person seeking to avoid liability.

17 Jones v Vernons Pools

The claimant submitted a correctly forecast pools coupon. The defendant had lost the coupon, but was able to rely on a clause in the coupon stating that 'the transaction was binding in honour only'.

Misrepresentation 10

Learning outcomes

Having studied this chapter you will be able to:

- Explain when the parties will be regarded as intending the agreement to be legally binding and how an agreement may be avoided because of misrepresentations

Syllabus context

In a misrepresentation situation, you must be able to identify (i) that all of the elements of a misrepresentation are in place, and (ii) which type of misrepresentation has been committed. It is important to establish the type of misrepresentation, as this has an effect on the type of remedies available and the source of those remedies.

Chapter overview

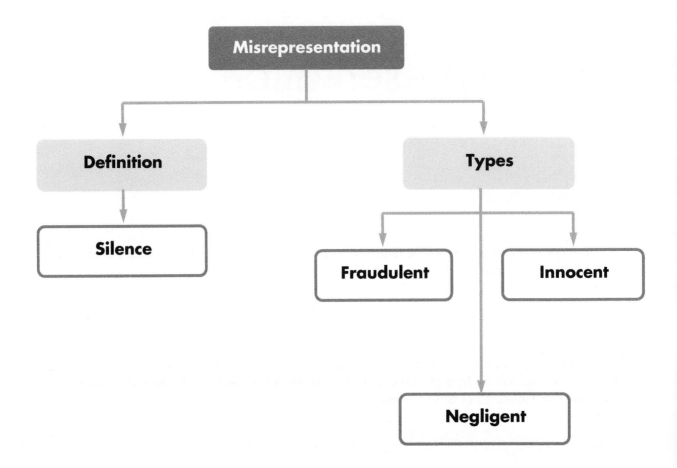

1 Definition of misrepresentation

Misrepresentations can be defined as 'a false **statement of fact** made by one party to the other **before the contract**, and made with a view to **inducing** the other party to enter into it'.

1.1 A contract will not be valid if either of the two parties did not genuinely consent to the contract. This may occur, for example, where one party makes a misrepresentation to the other in the course of negotiations.

1.2 It is important to note that not everything said prior to forming a contract will qualify as a potential misrepresentation. Specifically, the above definition excludes statements of opinion – *Bissett v Wilkinson* **(1)**.

1.3 As a general rule, **silence will not be a misrepresentation** unless the following circumstances prevail:

   (a)   An earlier statement made is no longer true

   (b)   An application is made for insurance

   (c)   Contracts made between parties in a fiduciary relationship, i.e. partnerships

Illustration 1

Harry agreed to sell his petrol station to Hermione in January, having told her that he sold at least 120,000 litres of petrol each year. By the time negotiations were completed, and contracts were signed in May, a local supermarket had opened up a petrol station on its site, which had the effect of reducing Harry's monthly petrol sales to 5,000 litres after it opened in March. Harry failed to disclose the opening of the new petrol station during the negotiations with Hermione.

The opening of the new petrol station has the effect of falsifying the statement made by Harry in January. His silence, when he had ample opportunity to correct the earlier statement constitutes a misrepresentation. Hermione can seek to have the sale set aside.

2 Types of misrepresentation

2.1

Type	Features	Remedies
Fraudulent	Knowingly making an untrue or reckless statement	Contract may be rescinded, or Damages claimed under the 'tort of deceit'
Negligent	Failing to take 'reasonable care' when making a false statement	Contract may be rescinded, or Damages claimed under the Misrepresentation Act 1967
Innocent	Genuinely believing a statement to be true	Contract may be rescinded, or damages claimed. If contract cannot be rescinded damages will not be awarded in *lieu*

2.2 It is not always practical or legally possible to seek rescission. The limitations, or bars, are:

(a) Contract has been affirmed

(b) Lapse of time (three yrs for personal injury claims, six yrs for contracts, 12 yrs for deeds)

(c) Restitution is not possible

(d) A third party has intervened (eg goods sold on to another person).

Illustration 2

Ritchie bought a second hand car in good faith, having been told by the seller, Mr Potts, that it had once been owned by the England football captain, Roy Rover. The illustrious ownership history of the car added £15,000 to its value when Ritchie bought it. Ritchie has now sold the car to his friend Fonzie, again at a premium of £15,000 to its market value. Ritchie had a genuinely held belief that Roy Rover was the car's original owner. Having taken the car to an expert valuer, Fonzie has now discovered that Mr Potts had falsified the log book records, and that Roy Rover had never owned the car.

In this case, Mr Potts has probably committed a fraudulent misrepresentation against Ritchie as evidenced by him knowingly falsifying the log book. As Ritchie has sold the car, he cannot claim to have the purchase contract rescinded as the car has been sold on. Instead, Ritchie should sue Mr Potts under the tort of deceit for £15,000. Alternatively, it may be easier for him to bring a claim under the Misrepresentation Act 1967, as the burden of proof is much lower.

Fonzie has been the victim of an innocent misrepresentation by Ritchie, so could either rescind the contract, and return the car to get his money back, or, keep the car and sue Ritchie for £15,000.

It could be argued that Ritchie has, in fact, committed a negligent misrepresentation as he could have taken steps to establish the veracity of Mr Pott's claim that Roy Rover had owned the car by ordering a search from the vehicle registration authorities.

Activity 1: Mispresentation

Luke is selling an old painting he has inherited from his mother, Padme. Luke knows the painting to be an imitation of 'The Degobah System' by the renowned artist, Skye Walker. Hans notices the painting, and certain it is the original, buys it for £250, believing it to be worth millions. When Hans get the painting valued, he is told it is practically worthless.

Required

Which of the following describes the legal situation between Luke and Hans?

A   Luke has committed a fraudulent misrepresentation
B   Luke has committed a negligent misrepresentation
C   Luke has committed an innocent misrepresentation
D   Luke has not committed any form of misrepresentation

Solution

Chapter summary

- A contract entered into following a **misrepresentation** is **voidable** by the person to whom the misrepresentation was made. A misrepresentation is a statement of fact, given before the contract is made, which is **untrue** and made by one party to the other in order to **induce** the latter to enter into the agreement.

- **Fraudulent misrepresentation** is a statement made knowing it to be untrue, not believing it to be true, or, careless as to whether it is true or false. Damages are claimed under the **tort of deceit**.

- **Negligent misrepresentation** is a statement made in the belief that it is true, but, without reasonable grounds for that belief. Damages are claimed under the **Misrepresentation Act 1967**

- **Innocent misrepresentation** is the residual category, being any statement made in the belief that it is true and with reasonable grounds for that belief. If the contract cannot be rescinded damages will not be awarded in *lieu*

Keywords

- **Misrepresentations** can be defined as 'a false statement of fact made by one party to the other before the contract, and made with a view to inducing the other party to enter into it'.

Activity 1: Mispresentation

D   Luke has done nothing wrong. He does not have a positive duty to inform Hans of his mistaken belief about the painting's authenticity.

Test your learning

1   As a general rule, silence cannot constitute misrepresentation.

True ☐

False ☐

2   A misrepresentation is:

(i)   A statement of fact which proves to be untrue

(ii)   A statement of law which proves to be untrue

(iii) Made by one party to the other before the contract is formed in order to induce the latter to enter into the contract

(iv)   A statement which affects the claimant's judgement

A   (ii) and (iv) only
B   (i), (iii) and (iv) only
C   (i), (ii), and (iv) only
D   All of the above

3   Damages for fraudulent misrepresentation are awarded under the Misrepresentation Act 1967.

True ☐

False ☐

M ⇒ B

B ⇒ K

4   Beyonce sold an antique vase to Kelly, honestly believing it to be from the Ming Dynasty. When she acquired the vase from Michelle it came with a certificate of authentication, a document that Kelly has just discovered is false. The vase is, in fact, an elaborate fake and is worthless. Which of the following statements are correct?

Beyonce has perpetrated a fraudulent misrep against Kelly ☐

Michelle may have committed an innocent misrep against Beyonce ☐

Kelly could rescind the contract and return the vase to Kelly ☐
Michelle
Beyonce

Beyonce may have perpetrated a negligent misrep against Kelly ☐

5   A misrepresentation is a statement of (1)...................., given (2)....................the contract is made, which is (3).................... and made by one party to the other in order to (4).................... the latter to enter into the agreement.

1 Bissett v Wilkinson

The plaintiff purchased from the defendant two blocks of land for the purpose of sheep farming. During negotiations, the defendant said that if the place was worked properly, it would carry 2,000 sheep. The plaintiff bought the place, believing that it would carry 2,000 sheep. Both parties were aware that the defendant had not carried on sheep-farming on the land. The Privy Council ruled that, in the absence of fraud, the purchaser had no right to rescind the contract.

Contract terms

Learning outcomes

Having studied this chapter you will be able to:

• Explain how the terms of a contract are established and their status determined

Syllabus context

In most contracts, there will be express terms, eg those that are commonly agreed orally or in writing, such as price. However in some, such as employment contracts, the vast majority of terms will be implied from other sources such as relevant legislation or established case law.

Chapter overview

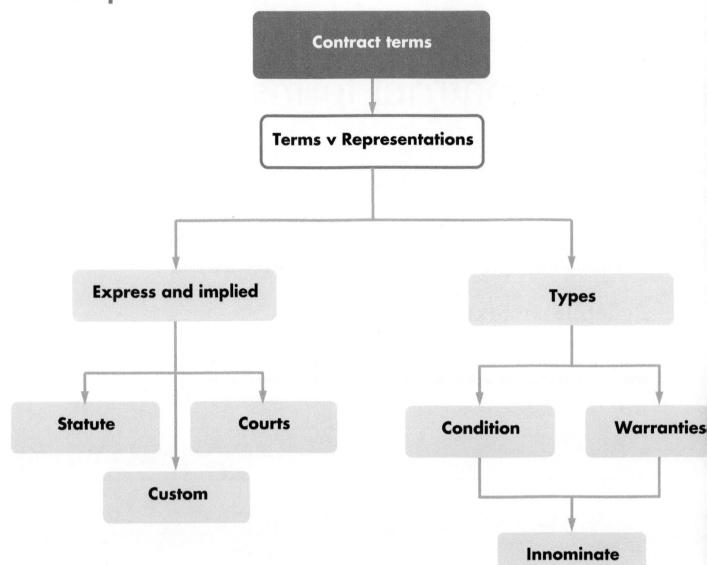

1 Terms v Representations

Key term

Some promises made during contract formation will not form part of the contract itself, but will merely act to induce the other party into the contract. Such pre-contractual statements are known as **representations**.

1.1 It is therefore important to be able to distinguish such statements from contractual terms, and this is done with the aid of four tests, as follows:

(a) If a statement is of **such importance** that the promisee would not have entered into the contract without it, it shall be deemed a term.

(b) Where there is a **time gap** between the statement and contract formation, the statement is more likely to be interpreted as a representation.

(c) If an oral statement is **omitted from a later written contract**, its exclusion will suggest that it was a representation.

(d) Should a party to the formation be an **expert**, or **possess special skills or knowledge**, statements made by them will be terms.

Illustration 1

Jensen was looking for a new sports car, and spotting several on the forecourt of his local dealer, 'Seb's Sports Cars', enquired about the mileage of a particularly sporty model. Seb replied that it had done only 2,000 miles since a replacement engine was fitted. Jensen agreed to buy the car on the spot. When getting the car insured, Jensen discovered that the car had, in fact, done 20,000 miles since the replacement engine was fitted.

In this instance, the courts would find the statement about the mileage to be a term of the contract, entitling Jensen to sue for breach of contract, not for a misrepresentation. As a car dealer, anything that Seb says can be relied upon by Jensen to be a term, owing to Seb's expertise and specialist knowledge.

2 Express and implied terms

Key term

Express term An express term is one that has been agreed by the parties between them, either orally or in writing, during the formation of a contract.

Implied terms are those terms that are not agreed upon by the parties, but are incorporated into the contract in one of the following ways:

(a) Implied by **statute** – such as the terms of the **Consumer Rights Act 2015**

(b) Implied by **custom** – some terms are customary through trade usage – *Hutton v Warren* **(1)**

(c) Implied by the **courts** – in order to give business efficacy to an agreement – *The Moorcock* **(2)**.

BPP
LEARNING MEDIA

Illustration 2

Marie buys a hairdryer from a high street retailer. The item comes with a 12 month guarantee from the manufacturer, per the warranty card inside the box. On the back of the shop receipt is a statement saying "In the event that you are not completely satisfied with this product it may be exchanged or returned for a full refund within 14 days – your statutory rights are not affected".

In this instance, Marie is benefiting from two express terms – the manufacturer's 12 month guarantee, and the money back promise from the retailer. Aside from this, there are implied terms revealed by the receipt, so called 'statutory rights'.

Activity 1: Express and implied terms

Gurjeet has recently started a job in a textiles factory. Before starting work, Gurjeet received a letter confirming the job offer, including details such as working hours and rates of pay, as well as a 16 page employee handbook detailing other company policies. During the job interview, Gurjeet was warned that there is a long-standing tradition in the industry that any losses caused due to poor workmanship are deducted from employee pay.

Required

Which of the following terms are governing the contract between Gurjeet and his employer?

(i)   Express
(ii)   Implied by statute
(iii) Implied by custom

A   (i) only
B   (i) and (iii)
C   (ii) and (iii)
D   (i) (ii) and (iii)

Solution

3 Types of term

Key term

A **condition** is a fundamental part of a contract; breach of a condition gives the innocent party the right to **repudiate** the contract **and** claim damages – *Poussard v Spiers* **(3)**.

A **warranty** is a lesser term that is deemed to be **collateral** to the main purpose of the contract. As such, a breach of warranty gives rise to a claim for damages only – *Bettini v Gye* **(4).**

Innominate terms are those that cannot be classified as a condition or a warranty until the contract has been breached. The test used to classify the term is whether or not the innocent party '**loses the whole of the benefit of the contract**' – *Aerial Advertising v Bachelors Peas* **(5)**.

Illustration 3

A contract for the sale of pulp pellets required them to be 'in good condition'. When the pellets were delivered, they were imperfect, and as such, the buyers rejected the cargo and refused to pay for them. The sellers needed to offload the pellets before they deteriorated further, and arranged to sell them at auction. At the auction, the original buyers bought the pellets, far below their original price, then proceeded to use them for their original purpose.

In this instance, the only grounds on which you could reject the cargo, and thus repudiate the contract, would be if there had been a breach of a condition – relating to the state of the pellets. As the buyers later used the pellets for their original purpose, clearly there was no 'loss of the whole of the benefit' and as such, the original breach of contract about the state of the pellets was a warranty, and not a condition. As such, the buyers had no right to repudiate the contract.

Activity 2: Contractual terms

Required

Which of the following statements concerning contractual terms are true?

(i)   Terms may be implied into contracts on the grounds of business efficacy.   T

(ii)   If a condition in a contract is not fulfilled, the whole contract is said to be discharged by breach.   T

(iii)   If a warranty in a contract is not fulfilled, the whole contract is said to be discharged by breach, but either party may elect to continue with his performance.   F

(iv)   Terms implied by custom override express terms on the same matter in the contract.   F

A   (i) and (ii) only
B   (iii) and (iv) only
C   (i), (ii) and (iv) only
D   All of the above

Solution

Chapter summary

- Statements made by the parties may be classified as **terms** or **representations**. Different remedies attach to breach of a term, and to misrepresentation respectively.

- As a general rule, the parties to a contract may include in the agreement whatever terms they choose. This is the principle of **freedom of contract**.

- Terms included in the contract are **express terms**. The law may complement or replace terms by implying terms into a contract.

- Terms may be **implied by the courts**, by **statute** or by **custom**.

- Statements which are classified as contract terms may be further categorised as **conditions** or **warranties**. A condition is a **vital** term going to the root of the contract, while a warranty is a term **subsidiary** to the main purpose of the contract. The remedies available for breach are different in each case.

- It may not be possible to determine whether a term is a condition or a warranty. Such terms are classified by the courts as **innominate** terms. The court will only construe a broken term as a condition or warranty if the parties' intentions when the contract was formed are very clear.

- A **condition** is a fundamental part of a contract; breach of a condition gives the innocent party the right to repudiate the contract and claim damages – *Poussard v Spiers (3)*.

- **Express term:** An express term is one that has been agreed by the parties between them, either orally or in writing, during the formation of a contract.

- **Implied terms:** are those terms that are not agreed upon by the parties, but are incorporated into the contract in one of the following ways:

  (a)   Implied by statute – such as the terms of the Consumer Rights Act 2015

  (b)   Implied by custom – some terms are customary through trade usage – *Hutton v Warren (1)*

  (c)   Implied by the courts – in order to give business efficacy to an agreement – *The Moorcock (2)*.

- **Innominate terms:** are those that cannot be classified as a condition or a warranty until the contract has been breached. The test used to classify the term is whether or not the innocent party 'loses the whole of the benefit of the contract' – *Aerial Advertising v Bachelors Peas (5)*.

- Some promises made during contract formation will not form part of the contract itself, but will merely act to induce the other party into the contract. Such pre-contractual statements are known as **representations**.

- A **warranty** is a lesser term that is deemed to be collateral to the main purpose of the contract. As such, a breach of warranty gives rise to a claim for damages only – *Bettini v Gye (4)*.

Activity answers

Activity 1: Express and implied terms

D   Gurjeet's contract contains Express terms – per the offer letter and handbook. Aside from this, there will be implied terms eg Health and Safety and Discrimination legislation, and there appears to be a Customary term around deductions for poor workmanship.

Activity 2: Contractual terms

A   Breach of a warranty does not discharge a contract. Terms implied by custom do not override express terms on the same matter.

1   A term may be implied into a contract by:

(i)   Statute

(ii)   Trade practice, unless an express term overrides it

(iii) The court, to provide for events not contemplated by the parties

(iv)   The court, to give effect to a term which the parties had agreed upon but failed to express because it was obvious

A   (ii) and (iii) only
B   (i), (ii) and (iv) only
C   (i), (ii) and (iii) only
D   (i), (iii) and (iv) only

2   **Fill in the blanks** in the statements below, using the words in the box.

A (1) .... is a vital term, going to the root of the contract, breach of which entitles the injured party to treat the contract as (2) .... and claim (3) ....

A (4) .... is a term (5) .... to the main purpose of the contract.

The consequence of a term being classified as innominate is that the court must decide what is the actual effect of its (6) ....

breach	condition	subsidiary
warranty	damages	discharged

3   Wario is a striker who plays for Liverbirds FC under a four year contract, which has two years to run. Unfortunately, Wario has been a major disappointment on the pitch and off it. He has now taken to only turn up to training when he fancies it, and refused to turn up to the last two matches when he was selected as a substitute. The manager of Liverbirds FC wants the club to sack Wario.

Which of the following accurately describes the club's legal position?

A   The club could claim damages from Wario
B   The club could repudiate Wario's contract
C   The club could repudiate Wario's contract and claim damages
D   The club is powerless to act

4   Which of the following statements is **inaccurate**?

   A   Conditions and warranties are the two basic types of express term

   B   A contract must expressly contain all essential terms

   C   A representation is something which induces the formation of a contract but which does not become a term of the contract

   D   Terms can be implied into a contract from trade practice or custom

5   DTZ Ltd has broken a contractual term contained in its contract with EVT Ltd. The term which has been broken is a warranty. Which of the following remedies are true remedies in this situation?

   EVT Ltd can recover damages from DTZ Ltd and avoid the contract.   True / False
   EVT may only recover damages   True / False
   EVT can consider the contract as repudiated   True / False
   EVT may consider the contract as repudiated or recover damages.   True / False

1 Hutton v Warren

It was held customary that a farm tenant could claim an allowance for seed and labour on quitting his tenancy.

2 The Moorcock

The owners of a wharf agreed that a ship should be moored alongside to unload its cargo. It was well known that at low tide, the ship would ground on the mud at the bottom. At low tide, the ship settled on a ridge concealed beneath the mud and suffered damage.

It was held that there was an implied term, though not expressed, that the ground alongside the wharf was safe at low tide since both parties knew that the ship must rest on it.

3 Poussard v Spiers

Failure to appear at performances when engaged as the lead role in an opera constituted a breach of condition, entitling the opera company to repudiate the contract and potentially to claim damages.

4 Bettini v Gye

Failure to appear at preliminary rehearsals only constituted a breach of warranty. The opera company was entitled to damages but not to repudiate the contract.

5 Aerial Advertising v Bachelors Peas

A contract to pay Aerial Advertising (AA) to fly over England trailing a banner saying 'Eat Bachelors Peas' has a clause stating 'the pilot must ring Bachelor Peas (BP) head office each day to inform the company about his flight plans for the day'. He did not telephone on the morning of November 11, and proceeded to make a flight over the crowded main square of Salford during the two minutes' silence, to the disgust and indignation of thousands of people assembled.

As a result, letters and telephone calls poured in upon BP, vigorously denouncing its conduct and announcing that its goods would be boycotted; and though it hastily inserted apologies in the local newspapers, BP alleged that the widespread public feeling and highly damaging press publicity had caused serious injury to its business, its goodwill, and the reputation of its dried peas. BP sued AA financial losses and repudiated the contract. AA protested, saying that whilst it would pay damages, the contract could be resumed in a few months.

It was held that on any other day of the year, the breach would have been of a warranty only, entitling BP to damages only. However, the severity of the adverse publicity was so great that in this instance, the term was classified as a condition, hence BP could end the contract.

Exclusion clauses

12

Learning outcomes

Having studied this chapter you will be able to:

- Explain how the terms of a contract are established and their status determined

Syllabus context

It is commonplace for businesses to supply their goods and services 'subject to terms and conditions'. A key 'T&C' often comes in the form of an exclusion clause. Such clauses are designed to afford the supplier legal protection via either a limitation, or, total exclusion of liability in the event that they breach the contract or are negligent.

The courts view these terms with great suspicion, so you will see in this topic the hurdles that the courts and legislators have created for exclusion clauses.

Chapter overview

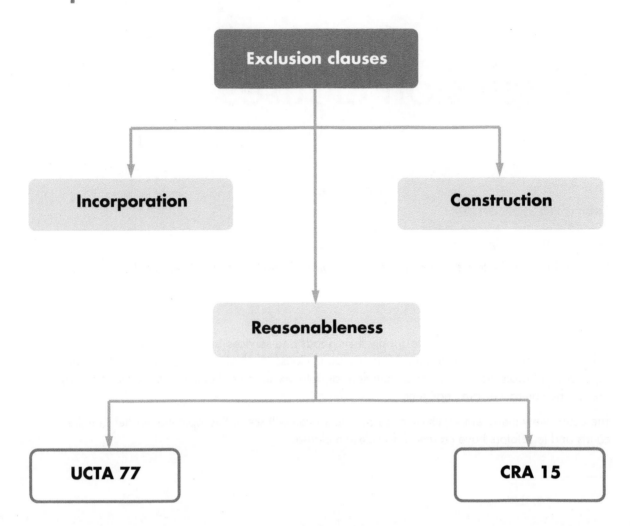

1 Exclusion clauses

Key term

> An **exclusion clause** can be described as 'any clause that attempts to exempt, or limit, the liability of one party for breach of contract or negligence'.

1.1 The courts are deeply suspicious of such clauses and as such, anyone wishing to enforce one would need to pass three tests:

(a) The clause needs to be **correctly incorporated** into the contract

(b) The clause needs to be **properly constructed**, in such a way that it is worded clearly to exclude the breach

(c) The clause is deemed **reasonable** per statute.

Illustration 1

Jurgen, a German citizen, handed his daughter some money to purchase a rail ticket for him as, given he cannot speak or read English, he wanted to ensure he got the right ticket. On the face of the ticket was printed 'Travel subject to our standard terms and conditions, see back"; and on the back, "Issued subject to the conditions and regulations in the company's timetables and notices.'

The conditions provided that excursion ticket holders should have no right of action against the company in respect of any injury, howsoever caused. Jurgen was injured when the train came to a sudden halt, having stood up to take his luggage from the overhead rack.

The legal issue is over whether or not Jurgen is bound by the T&C's that he cannot read. Case law would tell us that anyone who takes a ticket would be conscious that there would be some conditions and having regard to the impracticality of translating these into every language, they would be binding - in this case subject to being 'reasonable' in nature.

2 Incorporation – Case law rules

2.1 The first hurdle for any prospective clause to pass is whether or not it has been clearly incorporated into the contract before the contract is agreed. Incorporation can occur in three ways:

(a) By **signature** – once a document has been signed, parties are bound by its terms, irrespective of whether or not they have read them – *L'Estrange v Graucob* **(1).**

(b) By **notice** – any exclusion clause must be an integral part of the contract, and be given at the time that the contract is made. This extends to:

- Notice boards *Olley v Marlborough Court Hotel* **(2)**

- Tickets and receipts *Chapelton v Barry UDC* **(3)**

- Onerous clauses must be brought to attention *Thornton v Shoe Lane Parking* **(4)**

- Any verbal assurances given will overwrite a written clause *Curtis v Chemical Cleaning Co* **(5).**

(c) By custom – if it can be proved that through the ordinary course of dealings both parties were aware of the clause *Spurling v Bradshaw* **(6).**

3 Construction

3.1 The wording of the clause needs to be clear and precise. Any party attempting to rely on an ambiguous clause will be defeated per the **Contra Proferentum** rule – *Houghton v Trafalgar Insurance* **(7).**

3.2 Whilst it is possible to construct a clause designed to defeat the fundamental purpose of a contract, as per *Photo Productions v Securicor Transport* (8) such clauses are likely to be defeated by the statutory test of reasonableness.

4 Reasonableness – Statutory rules

Business – Business Contracts

4.1 The final test of whether an exclusion clause will stand in a business contract is that of reasonableness, as per the **Unfair Contract Terms Act 1977** (UCTA 77)

4.2 Although the Act regulates exclusion clauses in business-business contracts, certain contracts, such as those relating to insurance or transfer of an estate in land, are beyond its scope.

4.3 UCTA 77 works by determining whether a clause is void or subject to a test of reasonableness.

4.4 A clause is void in the following circumstances:

(a) A clause which purports to exclude or limit liability for **death or personal injury** resulting from negligence.

(b) In a contract for the sale or hire purchase of goods, a clause that purports to exclude the condition that the seller has a right to sell the goods.

4.5 A clause that is not void is subject to the statutory test of unreasonableness. In assessing **whether a clause is reasonable**, UCTA 77 directs a judge to consider the following factors:

(a) The relative bargaining strength of the parties

(b) Whether any inducement was accepted in waiver of rights

(c) Whether the customer had/ought to have had knowledge of the clause

(d) Whether the goods had been adapted or were for special order

(e) If failure to comply with a condition excludes or restricts the customer's rights.

4.6 The court's overriding consideration is whether or not in a given set of circumstances operation of the clause would be reasonable – *St Albans Council v International Computers* **(9).**

4.7 Business to consumer contracts are largely regulated by the Consumer Rights Act 2015, which is not examinable in BA4.

Activity 1: Wedding Days Ltd

'Wedding Days Ltd' are a company who provide a wedding car service. Their business standard terms and conditions contain a clause stating 'Wedding Days Ltd' accept no liability whatsoever for any property damage or personal injury howsoever caused'.

One customer, Peter, signed the terms and conditions and hired a car and driver for his daughter's wedding.

On the day of the wedding the driver stopped outside the church and helped negotiate the bride and her dress safely out of the car. Suddenly one of the hinges on the passenger door broke and the door slammed shut. This was as a result of negligent servicing of the car by Wedding Days Ltd. Unfortunately the tails of Peter's morning suit were caught in the door and caused a very noticeable rip in the material and his foot was trapped, breaking his big toe which meant he subsequently had to hobble up the aisle.

Required

(a) Is the clause part of the contract – if so why? ✓ Signed L'Est v Graucob

(b) Is it worded sufficiently to exclude liability for:

    (i) damage to the morning suit? - Yes - damage

    (ii) the broken toe? - Yes - p.i.

Solution

Chapter summary

- An **exclusion clause** may attempt to **restrict** one party's **liability** for breach of contract or for negligence.

- The courts protect parties from the harsher effects of exclusion clauses by ensuring that they are properly **incorporated** into a contract and then by **interpreting them strictly**.

- The **Unfair Contract Terms Act 1977** aims to protect parties when they enter into contracts by stating that some exclusion clauses are **void**, and considering whether others are **reasonable**.

- The **Consumer Rights Act 2015** provides protection for consumers in contracts with businesses.

Keywords

- An **exclusion clause** can be described as 'any clause that attempts to exempt, or limit, the liability of one party for breach of contract or negligence'.

Activity 1: Wedding Days Ltd

(a)   The contract is signed therefore it is incorporated. *L'Estrange v Graucob.*

(b)   (i)   Yes it covers damage to property as worded in the contract.

         (ii)   Yes it covers damage to the person as worded in the contract.

Whilst it is not on your syllabus it is worth briefly noting the effect of the Consumer Rights Act 2015 in this situation. Put simply the CRA 15 would apply a test of 'fairness' in this instance, and in the case of personal injury this would automatically be unfair, and the clause relating to the property damages would probably be rendered unfair, and therefore also unenforceable.

Test your learning

1 A business is classed as a consumer if it does not make the contract in the course of its business.

   True ☐

   False ☐

2 Match the laws to their jurisdictions under the law of contract

   (a) Common law   (1) Does not apply to business-to-consumer contracts

   (b) UCTA 1977   (2) Applies to all contracts

3 What is the 'main purpose' rule in relation to exclusion clauses?

   A   Exclusion clauses are intended to defeat the main purpose of a contact

   B   Exclusion clauses are not intended to defeat the main purpose of a contact

   C   The main purpose of an exclusion clause is to prevent one party from being liable for breach of contract

   D   The main purpose of an exclusion clause is to allocate risk between contracting parties

4 Which of the following describes the proper use of exclusion clauses?

   A   To limit an organisation's risk of being sued for causing personal injury
   B   To limit an organisation's risk of being sued for causing death
   C   To allocate risk between business organisations
   D   To hide onerous obligations on consumers in the 'small print'

5 In order to be binding on the consumer, an exclusion clause must be .... before the contract is formed. The wording must clearly exclude the breach in question; any attempt to rely on ambiguous terms will be defeated by the .... rule.

1 L'Estrange v Graucob

G purchased a slot machine from L. Contract excluded normal rights under the sale of goods act at the time. L signed the contract.

It was held that the conditions were binding on L, as she has signed them.

2 Olley v Marlborough Court

O paid for a hotel room in advance in reception. A notice disclaiming liability for loss of valuables was in the bedroom. Valuable furs were stolen from O's room.

It was held that the contract had been made when the room was paid for and the disclaimer came after. As such, it was too late and the hotel could not place any reliance on it.

3 Chapelton v Barry UDC

C hired a deckchair, paid, and received a ticket. The deckchair collapsed and C was injured. Notice disclaiming liability was on the back of the ticket.

The court held that the council was liable. The notice advertising deckchairs made no mention of the exclusion clause and it was not reasonable for them to communicate the exclusions on a receipt.

4 Thornton v Shoe Lane Parking

Thornton drove to the defendant's car park and was given a ticket by an automatic machine, which stated that it was issued, subject to conditions displayed inside the car park. The conditions inside the car park were in small print, and one of them excluded liability for damages to vehicles or injury to customers. Thornton was injured due partly to the defendant's negligence. Thornton was not held to be bound by the notice displayed inside the premises, as its existence was not made aware to him prior to paying.

5 Curtis v Chemical Cleaning Co

Curtis took her wedding dress to be cleaned and was asked to sign some conditions and when asked what they covered, was told that they excluded liability for damage to beads and sequins.

The clause actually disclaimed liability for any damage to the dress and when the dress was returned, it was badly stained. The Chemical Cleaning Co could not rely on their exclusion clause as they had misled Curtis as to its effect.

6 Spurling v Bradshaw

The defendant delivered eight barrels of orange juice to the claimants who were warehousemen. A few days later, the defendant received a document from the claimant which acknowledged receipt of the barrels. It also contained a clause exempting the claimants from liability for loss or damage "occasioned by the negligence, wrongful act or default" caused by themselves, their employees or agents. When the defendant collected the barrels, some were empty, and some contained dirty water. He refused to pay the storage charges and was sued by the claimants.

It was held that although the defendants did not receive the document containing the exclusion clause until after the conclusion of the contract, the clause had been incorporated into the contract as a result of a regular course of dealings between the parties over the years. The defendant had received similar documents on previous occasions and he was now bound by the terms contained in them.

7 Houghton v Trafalgar Insurance

Houghton's motor insurance company refused to pay out when the car was involved in an accident. The car had five seats but was carrying six passengers when it crashed. Trafalgar sought to avoid liability by relying on wording in the contract stating that liability was not accepted where the car was 'carrying an excess load'. The Court of Appeal ruled that 'excess load' could be interpreted as either too many passengers OR too much weight. Applying the *contra proferentum* rule, the latter interpretation was taken, defeating the defence of Trafalgar against the claim.

8 Photo Productions v Securicor Transport

S were engaged to guard P's premises. Contract contained an exclusion clause for damage caused by S's employees. S's employee deliberately started a fire which burnt the whole factory down. P argued that S could not rely on the clause as they had failed to perform their contracts to guard the premises.

It was held that total failure to perform a contract will not stop a party from relying on an exclusion clause – providing the clause is wide enough to cover the acts in question. In this case, it was felt to be so. The result of this case no longer forms a precedent as, per UCTA 77, the exclusion clause would be deemed unreasonable.

9 St Albans City and District Council v International Computers Ltd

St A employed ICL to assess the population of the city to base community charge. Clause in contract limited liability to £100K – although ICL has insurance cover of £50m. The database created by ICL was however inaccurate and St A lost £1.3m in revenue.

The clause was deemed unreasonable given the insurance held by ICL.

Forming the relationship 13

Learning outcomes

Having studied this chapter you will be able to:

- Explain how the contents of a contract of employment are established

Syllabus context

Most of us will be employed at some point in our lives. The law makes an important distinction between workers that are employed and those that are self-employed (independent contractors). It is crucial that you are able to distinguish between these types of workers, as they have different rights.

As an employee, you will be entitled to receive an employment contract. In a previous topic you will have learnt that the terms of this contract can be implied from a variety of sources outside of the written contract itself.

Finally, the contractual relationship is bilateral – the employee and employer owe each other a series of mutual obligations imposed by the common law and statute.

Chapter overview

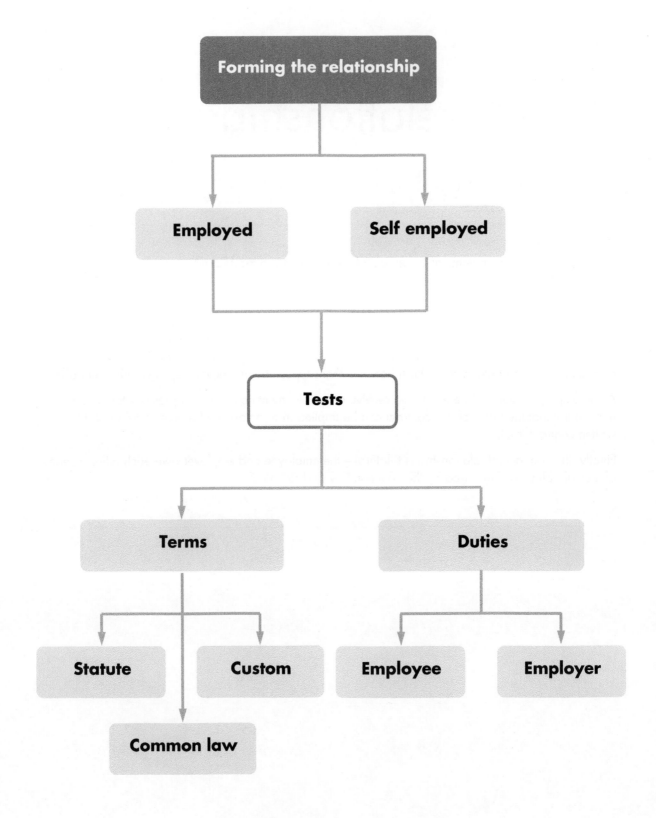

1 Employment status

1.1 Workers can be categorised as either of the following:

Employed works under a contact of service.

Self-employed works under a contract to provide services.

1.2 It is important to distinguish between the employment status of the two types of workers as their rights and obligations differ in the following areas:

    (a) Deduction and rates of taxation
    (b) Entitlement to sick/holiday pay
    (c) Rights upon dismissal
    (d) Liability for negligence
    (e) Provision of equipment
    (f) Registering for VAT purposes.

Illustration 1

Bonnie took her car into a local garage to have a new tyre fitted. Unfortunately, the trainee mechanic, Clyde, did not tighten the wheel nuts properly, and a few miles down the road, the wheel came loose and caused Bonnie to crash into a tree. Fortunately no one was hurt, but the car sustained significant damage.

In this instance, liability will fall on Clyde's employers, the garage owner. This is because, as a trainee mechanic, Clyde will be an employee, and as such, he benefits from 'vicarious liability', meaning his employer must indemnify him. For this reason, all employers are required by law to take out public liability insurance for a minimum amount of £5m and to display a valid certificate.

1.3 The status of a worker is not always immediately obvious and where this is the case, the following common law rules have been developed:

    (a) **Control test** – does the employer control what the employee does, and how they do it – *Walker v Crystal Palace FC* **(1).**

    (b) **Integration test** – where the control test is inconclusive, then it may be shown that the worker is fully integrated into the employers' business – *Cassidy v Ministry of Health* **(2).**

    (c) **Multiple test** – where the first two tests do not give a clear indication of a worker's status wider factors will be considered – *RMC v Ministry of Pensions* **(3)**:

        • Wearing of uniforms
        • Provision of tools
        • Holiday/sick pay entitlements
        • Use of substitute labour
        • Method of remuneration.

1.4 A further classification of worker is an agency worker. In determining whether the agency worker is effectively employed by the agency or the client at which they are placed, is determined by two factors:

(a) **Length of service** – being placed with one client for long enough can result in the worker becoming integrated into the client's workforce

(b) **Control over the worker** – where the client has sufficient control over the worker, they may become the ultimate employer.

Activity 1: Worker status

Required

Which of the following factors indicate that an individual is likely to be independent contractor rather than an employee?

EE A There is payment of a salary

EE B The 'employee' is not permitted to delegate his work

Indep C The 'employee' provides the necessary tools and equipment to perform the work

EE D There are 'mutual obligations' on the employer to provide, and the employee to perform, work

Solution

2 Contract formation

2.1 Although there are generally no formalities involved in forming the contract of employment, the **Employment Rights Act 1996** (ERA 96) stipulates that a written document, outlining the main terms of employment be supplied within **two months** of the date of commencement of employment. The particulars must include the following express terms:

(a) Job title and description
(b) Length of notice period
(c) Names of both parties and commencement date
(d) Rate and method of calculating pay
(e) Frequency of payment
(f) Holiday pay entitlements and rates
(g) Hours of work.

2.2 Additionally, the employment contract will be supplemented by terms implied from three main sources:

(a) **Statute**, such as the Equality Act

(b) **Common law**, such as the duties imposed on employees and employers discussed in Section 3 below

(c) **Custom**, for example, deductions for poor workmanship were commonplace in the cotton industry.

Activity 2: Employment contract

Required

Formation of a valid contract of employment requires

(i) Offer and acceptance
(ii) Intention to create legal relations
(iii) Consideration
(iv) A written document

A (i) and (ii) only
B (i), (ii) and (iii) only
C (ii) and (iii) only
D All of the above

Solution

3 Contractual duties

3.1 The law imposes the following duties on:

(a) **Employers – Common Law**

- Duty of mutual trust and confidence
- To pay wages
- To indemnify the employee
- To provide work for apprentices and piecemeal workers
- To provide for the health and safety of the employee.

(b) **Employers – Statute**

- Pay and equality – covering age, disability, sex, race, religion, pregnancy

- Provide itemised pay statements

- Time off work – trade union officials, redundant job seekers, public duties

- Time off work – maternity / paternity leave, ante-natal care, return to work

- Health and safety – Health and Safety at Work Act 1974.

(c) **Employees – Common Law**

- Fundamental duty of faithful service
- Reasonable competence
- Obedience
- Account for all monies and property
- Reasonable care and skill
- Personal service.

3.2 There is no duty to provide a reference when employees leave service. Indeed, employers may be liable under negligence for not taking reasonable care over accuracy and fairness if they volunteer to provide one.

Illustration 2

Peter worked in procurement for a company owned by his Uncle Ben. From time-to-time, Peter was offered substantial cash commissions from suppliers, keen to maintain their accounts with Ben's business. Peter considered these a perk of the job and used them to pay for family holidays.

When Ben discovered this, he sacked Peter on the spot, pointing out that with great power comes great responsibility. From a legal standpoint, Ben is justified in this as Peter failed to account for the commissions and breached his common law duties.

Activity 3: Common law duties

Required

Which of the following are common law duties owed by employees?

To pay wages	☒
To provide a reference	☒
Obedience	☑
Personal service	☑
Time off work	☒
Reasonable competence	☑

Solution

Chapter summary

- It is important to distinguish between a **contract of service** (employment) and a **contract for services** (independent contractor). Each type of contract has different rules for taxation, health and safety provisions, protection of contract and vicarious liability in tort and contract.

- A contract of service is distinguished from a contract for services, usually because the parties **express the agreement** to be one of service. This does not always mean that an employee will not be treated as an independent contractor by the court, however; much depends on the three tests:
  - Control test
  - Integration test
  - Economic reality test.

- The **distinction** between employed and self-employed is important as to whether certain rights are available to an individual and how they are treated for tax purposes.

- There are **no particular legal rules** relating to the **commencement** of employment – it is really just like any other contract in requiring offer and acceptance, consideration and intention to create legal relations.

- The employer has an **implied duty** at common law to take reasonable care of his employees; he must select proper staff, materials and provide a safe system of working.

- The **employee has a duty** of faithful service and to exercise care and skill in performance of his duties.

- **Statutes imply terms** into employment contracts, which may not usually be overridden, regarding pay, maternity leave and work-life balance generally, time off, health and safety and working time.

- Contracts of employment can **only be varied if the contract expressly** gives that right, or if all parties consent to the variation.

- **Vicarious liability** means liability for the torts of others and arises because of a relationship between the parties.

Keywords

- **Employed:** works under a contact of service.
- **Self-employed:** works under a contract to provide services.

Activity 1: Worker status

C   Where the 'employee' provides their own tools and equipment it can indicate that they are an independent contractor. However, other factors would be taken into account too. The other options are clear indications of a contract of service.

Activity 2: Employment contract

B   A valid employment contract does not have to be a written document. A written outline of the main terms of the contract must, however, be supplied within two months of commencement.

Activity 3: Common law duties

The correct options are Obedience, Personal service and Reasonable competence. The other options are duties owed by the employer, though in terms of a reference, there is no duty on the employer to supply one.

Test your learning

1   What tests are applied by the courts to answer these questions?

- Has the employer control over the way in which the employee performs his duties?   (1) ....

- Is the skilled employee part of the employer's organisation? (2) ....

- Is the employee working on his own account? (3)....................

2   An employee who starts work is told he is not entitled to an itemised payslip until he has worked for two months.

True   ☐

False   ☐

3   Which of these options are open to an employer who wishes to vary the terms of an employment contract?

(i)   Produce a wholly new contract
(ii)   Vary the terms without changing the contract
(iii) Change the existing contract

A   (i) and (ii) only
B   (ii) and (iii) only
C   (iii) only
D   All of the above

4   Which of the following is **NOT** an implied duty of an employer?

A   To pay a reasonable wage
B   To provide a reasonable reference
C   To ensure a safe working environment
D   To reimburse expenses incurred in the course of employment

5   Delete where applicable

- The employer is vicariously liable for the employee's torts **in the course of his employment/at any time**.

- Employers are **liable/not liable** if an employee commits a tort whilst disobeying instructions during the course of their work.

- Employers are **liable/not liable** for torts committed in a company vehicle when the employee is undertaking private business.

- Employers are **liable/not liable** when an employee defrauds a client to his own advantage in the course of his employment.

1 Walker v Crystal Palace FC

As a professional football player, Walker claimed to be self-employed. However, it was ruled that he was employed under a contract of service as he was subject to the control of his master in the form of training, discipline and method of pay.

2 Cassidy v Ministry of Health

In determining for the purposes of vicarious liability whether or not surgeons were employed or self-employed Lord Denning decreed:

'In my opinion authorities who run a hospital, be they local authorities, government boards, or any other corporation, are in law under the self-same duty as the humblest doctor; whenever they accept a patient for treatment, they must use reasonable care and skill to cure him of his ailment. The hospital authorities cannot, of course, do it by themselves; they have no ears to listen through the stethoscope, and no hands to hold the surgeon's knife. They must do it by the staff which they employ; and if their staff are negligent in giving the treatment, they are just as liable for that negligence as is anyone else who employs others to do his duties for him.....'

Having stated therefore that the surgeon was an employee of the hospital, it was the hospital that was held vicariously liable for his negligent acts.

3 RMC v Ministry of Pensions

Following a query over national insurance contributions, the question arose as to whether RMC's drivers were employed or independent contractors. The court looked at multiple factors to decide: drivers were buying their own lorries on HP from RMC; they were responsible for maintenance; they were paid on deliveries made; there was no provision for holidays or fixed hours of work; substitute drivers were allowed; the drivers wore company overalls. Considering all these factors, the court held that drivers were *not* employees.

Policies and practices 14

Having studied this chapter you will be able to:

- Explain what work place policies and procedures are required legally or recommended as best practice

Syllabus context

The employment contract is one of the most tightly regulated contracts, informed by statute, common law and, occasionally custom. The overriding theme of this regulation is the protection of the worker, whether it be ensuring continuity of conditions upon a transfer of undertaking, or the myriad of rules that outlaw discrimination in all its forms.

Within this is the regulation of health and safety (H&S). H&S is a high profile area of law and for this exam, you will need to understand the duties this imposes on the employee and employer as well as the remedies available for breach.

Finally, we look at other relevant issues, including a number of areas of corporate crime, such as bribery and money laundering. Aside from these, there are other areas that employers need to be aware of, such as the rights of whistle-blowers, the need to protect and secure data as well as the increasing impact of social media use within the workplace.

Chapter overview

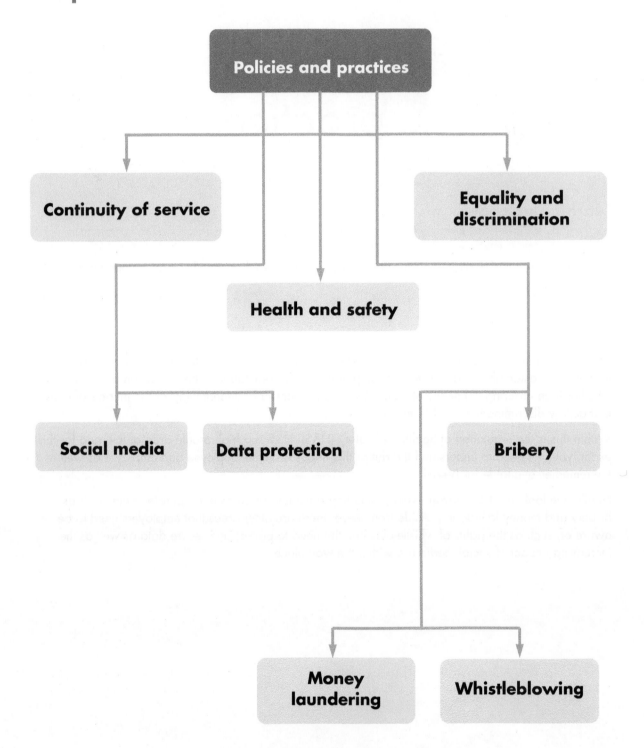

1 Continuity of service

1.1 Many of the rights that employees have are contingent upon having sufficient length of continuous service eg two years for redundancy payments.

1.2 When calculating length of service the following rules are applied:

(a) A week is one in which the employee worked for at least 8 hours

(b) Some periods of absence are included eg sick leave

(c) If the employee has worked in the same business before its transfer to his present employer, his previous service may be counted.

1.3 **TUPE** (Transfer of Undertakings (Protection of Employment)) states that when an undertaking is transferred, the employees of the business are automatically transferred (on the same terms and with unbroken service) to the employment of the new owner, provided that:

(a) There is a real change in ownership of the business
(b) There must be continuity in the business before and after the transfer.

A new employer may vary terms if there are economic, technical or organisational reasons to justify this.

1.4 Any dismissal in connection with TUPE gives rise to a claim for unfair dismissal.

Activity 1: TUPE

Required

Ross works for the Little Coffee Shop Ltd, which has just been acquired by the Mega Coffee Corporation plc. Under the TUPE regulations, Ross has the right to:

A Demand a new contract on exactly the same terms and conditions that he currently works under

B Receive redundancy payment if he decides to resign

C Resign and claim unfair dismissal

D Carry forward his employment with the Little Coffee Shop Ltd as continuous employment

= EK can vary y has E,T,O reason

Solution

2 Equality and discrimination

2.1 Employees are protected against discrimination at work by the following pieces of statute.

2.2 **The Equality Act** outlaws discrimination subjecting any prejudicial practices to the test of 'justification'.

2.3 Justification is assessed against the following criteria:

- **Proportionate** – the discriminatory effects are outweighed by other benefits

- **Legitimate** – for reasons relating to business efficacy or health and safety.

2.4 The legislation covers both direct and indirect discrimination:

- **Direct discrimination** – treating people less favourably than others because of a protected characteristic.

- **Indirect discrimination** – applying a provision or practice which disadvantages people with a certain protected characteristic and which is not objectively justifiable.

Illustration 1

Angelina applied to join the armed response unit of her police force. Having passed the initial physical and mental examinations, she is dismayed that she is unable to participate in the basic shooting test as the standard issue firearm is too large for her to use. Although she is of above average height for a woman, Angelina is unable to pull the trigger as her hand and fingers are simply not large enough, and consequently, she has been kicked off the programme.

Angelina has a strong case for indirect discrimination, the police force's choice of weapon clearly discriminates against people with smaller hands, a characteristic most likely to found amongst female candidates. The force should reinstate Angelina and either change the standard issue firearm, or provide a suitable alternative.

2.5 **Sex discrimination** has been outlawed since 1975, with a series of regulations and legislations making it unlawful to discriminate directly or indirectly on the basis of gender.

2.6 The law in this area extends to:

- Advertising posts
- Selection of candidates
- Promotion and training
- Dismissal.

2.7 It is, however, lawful to discriminate where a person's sex is a '**genuine qualification for a job**' including:

- Characteristics – modelling
- Authenticity – actors
- Decency/privacy.

2.8 Similar laws exist to outlaw **racial discrimination**, covering colour, race, nationality or ethnic or national origins at all stages of employment. Again, there are exceptions made for genuine occupational qualifications such as:

- Authenticity in entertainment
- Personal welfare services
- Maintaining ethnic authenticity in a bar or restaurant.

Disability

2.9 Protection is afforded to disabled workers. Any situation where an individual is treated less favourably, for a reason related to disability, is deemed to be discriminatory.

2.10 The effect of the legislation is to require an employer to make '**reasonable adjustments**'.

2.11 Other anti-discriminatory laws include:

- Equal pay – for men and women engaged in 'like work'

- Sexual orientation – covering all forms of sexual orientation

- Age – workers can no longer be required to retire at the statutory retirement age, nor used as justification for redundancy

- Trade unions – workers cannot be forced to join, or barred from joining official unions.

2.12 Applications for discrimination must be made to the employment tribunal within three months. The tribunal has the following powers:

- Compensation
- Recommend the employer takes corrective action
- Appoint ACAS to arbitrate between the parties.

2.13 The tribunal cannot:

- Force the employer to promote someone
- Insist the employer takes on a job applicant.

Activity 2: Discrimination

Required

David attends a job interview in his wheelchair, and is shocked to be told by the interviewer that he is not suited to the job as the company was ideally looking to recruit a female candidate as the role involved counselling female victims of domestic abuse. This requirement was included in the detailed job description which David had failed to read properly.

Has David been discriminated against?

Directly ☑

Indirectly ☐

Could the employer justify discriminating against David when awarding the job?

Yes ☑

No ☐

Solution

Diversity

2.14 The aim of **diversity** is to focus on maximising the potential of all staff. This broadens the discrimination agenda into something positive that relates to all employees rather than just disadvantaged groups.

2.15 The concept of diversity can be extended to recognise and make use of the unique characteristics of a particular group. An organisation will need to be proactive in managing the needs of a diverse workforce in areas (beyond the requirements of equal opportunity and discrimination regulations) such as:

(a) Tolerance of individual differences

(b) Communicating effectively with (and motivating) ethnically diverse workforces

(c) Managing workers with increasingly diverse family structures and responsibilities

(d) Managing the adjustments to be made by an increasingly aged workforce

(e) Managing increasingly diverse career aspirations/patterns, flexible working etc

(f) Dealing with differences in literacy, numeracy and qualifications in an international workforce

(g) Managing co-operative working in ethnically diverse teams.

3 Health and safety

3.1 The Health and Safety at Work Act 1974 imposes the following duties on:

(a) **Employers**

- Make suitable and sufficient assessments of the risks likely to arise
- Appropriate measures to reduce these risks
- To issue personal protective equipment
- To provide safety training and information
- To keep records of accidents and testing of equipment
- To form a safety committee if requested by a trade union representative.

(b) **Employees**

- Take reasonable care of themselves and others
- Allow the employer to carry out his or her duties (including enforcing safety rules)
- Not interfere intentionally or recklessly with any machinery or equipment
- Inform the employer of any situation which may be a danger
- To use all equipment properly.

3.2 As 'strangers' to the working environment, **contractors** need to communicate closely with managers to foresee and guard against hazards.

3.3 **Safety representatives** are appointed, normally by their trade union, to inspect the workplace from a health and safety perspective. The employer has a legal duty, where a safety representative exists, to co-operate with them.

3.4 **Enforcement** of the Act is by the **Health and Safety Commission**, which is empowered to do the following:

- To enter and investigate a workplace
- To issue improvement notices, requiring remedial action within a stated time period
- To issue prohibition notices, ordering the cessation of certain activities.

3.5 **Employees may bring civil action** against their employer for any failure to observe H&S legislation.

Tom and his brother, Jerry were highly trained explosives experts. They were selected to detonate an explosion in a quarry so that the rubble could be processed for valuable minerals. The brothers had received extensive training and signed a waiver absolving their employer, EyeSeaEye (ESE) of any liability in the event of an accident. The brothers decided it would be fun to throw a small explosive charge at each other, but unfortunately the charge exploded, blinding Tom. Tom is now suing ESE for a breach of H&S regulations.

Required

Which of the following statements represents the likely outcome of Tom's legal action?

A   Tom's claim will succeed, ESE failed to provide Tom with personal protective equipment

B   Tom's claim will fail as Tom and Jerry failed to **take reasonable care of themselves and others**

C   Tom's claim will succeed, ESE failed to take appropriate measures to reduce these risks

D   Tom's claim will fail as the waiver protects ESE against legal action

Solution

4 Bribery

4.1 Bribery offences are regulated by the Bribery Act 2010 which came into force on the 1st July 2011. The Act created four classes of offence:

(a) Bribing another person (active bribery)

(b) Receiving a bribe (passive bribery)

(c) Bribing a foreign public official

(d) Corporate failure to prevent bribery, where a company or partnership fails to put in place 'adequate procedures' to prevent offences being committed by an employee, agent or subsidiary

Illustration 2

Sweett Group PLC ("Sweett"), a UK-listed provider of professional services for the construction sector, has become the first company to be sentenced and convicted for the corporate offence of failing to prevent bribery. The case illustrates the far-reaching extra-territorial effect of the Bribery Act and emphasises the need for UK-connected corporates to exercise strong oversight over their global operations.

Following media allegations in June 2013, Sweett began an internal investigation. As a result, it identified and reported two suspicious contracts to the Serious Fraud Office ("SFO"). The SFO began its own investigation into the AIM-listed company in July 2014. It concluded that one of Sweett's Middle Eastern subsidiaries had made corrupt payments to Khaled Al Badie, a senior Emirati official at Al Ain Ahlia Insurance Company, in order to secure a contract to consult on the development of the Rotana Hotel in Abu Dhabi.

In December 2015, Sweett admitted failing to prevent bribery. The company was sentenced at Southwark Crown Court with a total penalty of £2.25 million imposed.

Eversheds 2016

4.2 The Act makes it clear that bribery can be committed by both state and privately employed persons and that the scope extends to offences committed outside of the UK.

4.3 Specific defences are available to members of the armed forces and the secret services when engaged on active duty.

4.4 A general defence is one of having 'adequate procedures'. Whilst this term is not defined in the Act, the guidance provided indicates that companies are expected to formulate policies on gifts (including a gift register) and provide staff training.

4.5 The maximum penalty under the Act is 10 years imprisonment and/or unlimited fine.

Bonny and Clive run a small accounting practice and undertake the following transactions:

Bonny took three prospective clients to an international rugby match, providing match tickets, food and drink in the hope of winning their business.

Clive met with a local tax inspector and offered him a pair of centre court tickets at Wimbledon if he would 'turn a blind eye' to a minor irregularity in the financial records of a new client acquired by Bonny's trip to the rugby.

Required

Which of the following correctly describes the position of Bonny and Clive in respect of the Bribery Act?

A   Neither Bonny nor Clive have committed an offence

B   Bonny is guilty of bribery, Clive is not

C   Bonny is not guilty of bribery, Clive is

D   Both Bonny and Clive have committed an offence of bribery

Solution

---

5 Money Laundering

Key term

Money laundering	is the process by which the proceeds of crime, which have illegitimate origins, are converted into assets that appear to be legitimate.

5.1   The process usually comprises of three distinct phases:

(a)   **Placement** – the disposal of the proceeds of crime into an apparently legitimate business property or activity

(b)   **Layering** – the transfer of money from place to place, in order to conceal its criminal origins

(c)   **Integration** – the culmination of placement and layering, giving the money the appearance of being from a legitimate source

5.2   Money laundering was first made a criminal offence in the UK under the Drug Trafficking Offences Act 1986, but is now regulated by the Proceeds of Crime Act 2002 (PCA 02) amongst others.

5.3 The PCA 02 has defined three categories of offence, these being:

(a) **Laundering** – being the offences of concealing, disguising, converting, transferring, or removing criminal property from the UK

(b) **Failure to report** – it is an offence for someone who knows or suspects that another person is engaged in money laundering not to report that fact to the appropriate authority. This offence only relates to individuals working in a regulated industry, eg accountants

(c) **Tipping off** – it is an offence to make a disclosure likely to prejudice a money laundering offence already being undertaken, or which may be undertaken.

5.4 The penalties for those found guilty of money laundering are:

(a) Laundering – a maximum 14 year prison sentence is possible, and/or a fine. Additionally, the police may seize the illegitimate assets

(b) Failure to report - punishable by a maximum five year sentence, and/or a fine

(c) Tipping off - punishable by a maximum five year sentence, and/or a fine.

Activity 5: Luigi and Mario

Luigi works as a bookkeeper for a small accounting firm, and suspects that one of his most valuable clients, and best friends, Mario is laundering money through his ice-cream parlour business. Concerned that Mario could land himself in trouble after noticing that the tax authorities were starting to take a closer than normal look at the books of the ice-cream parlour Luigi emailed Mario saying:

'Mario, not sure if your ice-cream parlour is 100% legitimate, but I'd say for the foreseeable future you should stick to selling cones and lollies only, if you know what I mean.'

Required

Which of the following offences has Luigi committed. Select all that apply.

A Money laundering → *query how involved in ice-cream parlour a/cs*

B Tipping off

C Bribery

D Failure to report

Solution

6 Data Protection

6.1 The Data Protection Act 1998 (DPA) aims to protect individuals not companies (Data subjects) from misuse of information being held on computer-based and manual information systems by data controllers.

6.2 The Act applies to personal data ie data which may identify an individual. This includes facts and opinions about the data subject and intentions of the data controller.

6.3 In order to protect the data subject, the DPA sets out the following eight principles which data controllers must comply with:

    (a)   Lawful processing

    (b)   Lawful purpose

    (c)   Relevant, not excessive

    (d)   Accurate

    (e)   Length of time

    (f)   Rights, meaning personal data must be used in accordance with the Act

    (g)   Technical and organisational measures to be taken against unlawful processors

    (h)   Transfer outside European Economic Area is strictly controlled.

6.4 The DPA also sets out the following rights for the data subject:

    (a)   Access data held about them

    (b)   Avoidance of damage, by preventing processing likely to cause harm

    (c)   Junk mail, preventing use for direct marketing

    (d)   Automatic decisions, to request no data is used for automatic decisions that materially affect the data subject

    (e)   Compensation for contravention of the act

    (f)   Action against inaccurate data

    (g)   Right to ask the Information Commissioner to assess if DPA has been contravened.

6.5 There are certain data which are exempt from the DPA including the following:

    (a)   Payroll and accounts

    (b)   Examination scripts

    (c)   Personal data held by unincorporated members' clubs

    (d)   Domestic data

    (e)   Research where data does not identify data subject and is not used for any other purpose

    (f)   Data relating to crime prevention and national security

    (g)   Confidential references given by data controllers.

Illustration 3

TV presenter Jeremy Clarkson lost money after publishing his bank details in his newspaper column. The former Top Gear host revealed his account numbers after rubbishing the furore over the loss of 25 million people's personal details on two computer discs. He wanted to prove the story was a fuss about nothing. But Clarkson admitted he was wrong after he discovered a reader had used the details to create a £500 direct debit to the charity, Diabetes UK.

Clarkson published details of his bank account in his weekly newspaper column, including details of his account number and sort code. He even told people how to find out his address. Clarkson acknowledged his mistake in his next column, pointing out that the Data Protection Act itself prevented the bank from telling him who had set up the direct debit on his behalf.

Activity 6: Data protection

Sarah Conner is a data subject of Pest Exterminators Ltd. She has asked to see the information held about her by the company in its personnel files. In doing so, she discovers that the data was inaccurate, as it had not been updated to reflect the fact that she has remarried and changed her name. She is also cross that the company has refused to show her its payroll records, as she is convinced that she is being paid less than a colleague of hers, Arnie.

Required

Which TWO of the following statements are true?

A) The company faces a potential criminal liability for maintaining inaccurate data

✗ B The company is bound to pay Sarah compensation in respect of the *– only y suffered* inaccuracy *a loss*

✗ C Sarah can demand access to the company's payroll records *– exempt*

D) Sarah can demand that the company correct the data action

Solution

7 Whistleblowing

> **'Whistleblowing'** is the name commonly given to workers making a disclosure of wrongdoing (usually) by their employer.

7.1 The relevant legislation is the Public Interest Disclosure Act 1998 (PIDA).

7.2 The protection is afforded to workers generally (and not just to 'employees') and there is no requirement as to age or length of service.

7.3 In order to receive protection under PIDA, the worker must make a qualifying disclosure in the public interest to an appropriate person.

> ## Illustration 4
>
> *Goode v Marks & Spencer* – Mr Goode was an employee of 25 years of Marks and Spencer (M&S). He was sacked for gross misconduct after passing an internal email outlining proposals to reduce redundancy benefits by up to 25% to a newspaper. Mr Goode's suspension sparked a public row that proved embarrassing for both the retailer the group's chief executive.
>
> Goode claimed he passed on the internal memo outlining proposals to cut redundancy benefits because he felt that the internal consultation process that the company was undertaking about the plans was a 'sham'.
>
> Mr Goode's plea that his sacking was a breach of human rights was rejected as insufficient grounds for making the disclosure. Crucial to the case was the fact that M&S's plans were only in outline at the time and no decision on implementation had been taken.

7.4 A disclosure is a qualifying disclosure if, in the reasonable belief of the worker making it, the information disclosed tends to show one or more of the following:

   (a) That a criminal offence has been committed, is being committed or is likely to be committed

   (b) That a person has failed, is failing or is likely to fail with any legal obligation to which he is subject

   (c) That a miscarriage of justice has occurred, is occurring or is likely to occur

   (d) That the health and safety of an individual has been, is being or is likely to be endangered

   (e) That the environment has been, is being or is likely to be damaged

   (f) That information tending to show any matter falling within these categories has been, is being or is likely to be deliberately concealed.

7.5 The wrongdoing disclosed is commonly done by the employer but a disclosure could also be made about the acts of fellow workers.

7.6 The test of reasonable belief is a subjective one that is specific to the worker making the disclosure. Where disclosing something that is 'likely to occur' objective evidence must be produced rather than a mere expression of an opinion.

7.7 The public interest term was introduced in 2013, but is not defined. Alongside this change was the repeal of the requirement to make disclosures in good faith. Where a disclosure is made in bad faith, the employee is still afforded protection under PIDA 98; however, any award of damages may be reduced by up to 25%.

7.8 In order to be a protected disclosure, the disclosure must be to one of the persons specified by the Act:

(a) Legal adviser in the course of obtaining legal advice
(b) Employer or another responsible person
(c) Minister of the crown
(d) Prescribed bodies such as Health and safety executive, HMRC or FSA
(e) Media, police or MPs, so long as not for personal gain.

7.9 Workers who have made a protected disclosure have the right not to suffer a detriment, such as lack of promotion, lack of training or opportunity, unjustified disciplinary action, pay issues or failure to renew contracts as a result of having made a protected disclosure.

7.10 An 'employee' who is dismissed or selected for redundancy for having made a protected disclosure shall be regarded as having been automatically unfairly dismissed. Any gagging clause in conflict with the Act will be void.

Activity 7: Whistleblowing

In some cases, a worker may intend to disclose wrongdoing by his employer to someone outside the workplace, for example, the police. In such cases, the disclosure will be protected by the Public Interest Disclosure Act 1998 if it is reasonable in all the circumstances and is not made for personal gain. In addition, the worker will need to satisfy one of several other criteria in order to receive the protection of the Act (assuming that the matter disclosed is a qualifying disclosure within the Act).

Required

Which one of the following is NOT one of those criteria and will not, therefore, afford the statutory protection?

A   The fact that he had already raised the matter internally

B   Reasonably believing that a cover-up was likely and there was no prescribed person to whom disclosure could be made

C   Reasonably believing that he would be victimised if he raised the matter internally

D   The fact that the matter was of a serious criminal nature

Solution

8 Social Media

8.1 The rise of social media sites has created three issues for employers:

    (a)   Productivity concerns

    (b)   IT security risks

    (c)   Privacy concerns.

8.2 **Productivity** can be adversely affected by staff spending excessive amounts of time updating their social media profile, or reading other peoples' posts. This is sometimes referred to as '**time theft**'.

8.3 To combat time theft, employers may start to restrict or monitor staff internet usage, though such measures risk creating mistrust and damaging staff morale.

8.4 **IT security** risks relate to staff inadvertently downloading malicious software on their computers, and putting the whole company's IT infrastructure at risk.

8.5 **Privacy concerns** relate to the degree to which a company can monitor employee use of social media. For instance, it is common for employers to scan the social media postings of prospective employees, blurring the lines between an employee's professional and personal life.

Illustration 5

In 2013, Australian cricketer David Warner was fined by his employer (Cricket Australia) for inappropriate 'Tweets' made when he became embroiled in a Twitter row with two Australian cricket journalists.

Also in 2013, in the UK, a 17-year-old female resigned as Kent police youth commissioner because of comments she had made in the past on social media. Kent police admitted the new recruit's Twitter and Facebook accounts had not been checked ahead of her appointment, but stated that social media checks would now become part of their recruitment process.

8.6 **ACAS** has issued the following guidance to employers:

    (a)   Develop a **policy** for social media usage in the workplace

    (b)   **Educate** employees, specifically on what constitutes reasonable usage

    (c)   Issue **guidelines** to line managers on how to manage **homeworkers**

    (d)   Settle in **new staff** with training on acceptable social media usage

    (e)   **Disciplinary measures** should be made clear and enacted where necessary.

Chapter summary

- Certain employment rights are **only available** if an employee has a specified period of continuous employment.

- **Statutes imply** terms into employment contracts to prohibit **discrimination** in various categories. In addition to the longstanding legislation preventing discrimination on grounds of **sex** or **race**, there is new legislation which expands the framework considerably.

- The **Health and Safety at Work Act** 1974, it is the duty of every employer, as far as is practicable, to ensure the health, safety and welfare of all employees. In particular, they should

    - Provide and maintain plant and systems of work which are safe and without risk

    - Make arrangements to ensure health and safety in relation to the use, **handling**, **storage** and **transport** of articles and substances

    - Provide adequate **information**, **instruction**, **training** and **supervision**

    - Maintain **safe places** of work

    - Ensure there is **adequate access** in and out

    - Provide a safe and healthy working environment.

- The responsibility for making health and safety regulations rests on the government. A **Health and Safety Commission** oversees the working of the system. Its members include representatives of employers' organisations and of trade unions.

- It is an **offence** for an individual to make or **accept bribes**, in public or private companies, in the UK and worldwide.

- It is also an offence for a company to **fail to take reasonable steps to avoid** its employees committing bribery offences.

- **Money laundering** is the three step process of converting the proceeds of crime into apparently legitimate assets. This involves **placing**, **layering** and **integrating**.

- There are three offences that can be committed, **laundering**, **failing to report** and **tipping-off**.

- The **Data Protection Act** sets out the eight data protection principles, simultaneously giving rise to eight rights for data subjects.

- Some data is exempt from the Act, notably payroll and examination records.

- **Whistleblowers** are protected from dismissal or discrimination in the workplace via the **Public Information Disclosures Act**. This extends to qualifying disclosures, made in the public interest, to an appropriate person.

- **Social media** creates issues for employers around **productivity, IT security** and **privacy**. ACAS has issued guidance to employers to assist them with performance management and social media.

Keywords

- **Money laundering:** is the process by which the proceeds of crime, which have illegitimate origins, are converted into assets that appear to be legitimate.

- **'Whistleblowing':** is the name commonly given to workers making a disclosure of wrongdoing (usually) by their employer.

Activity 1: TUPE

D   Options B and C are untrue. Option A is incorrect as the new employer may vary terms if there are economic, technical or organisational reasons.

Activity 2: Discrimination

Directly – the advert expressly mentions gender.

Yes – The employer could argue that the sensitivity of the job would mean that only a woman could do the job effectively. This could, however, be contested by David on the grounds of proportionality and legitimacy.

Activity 3: Tom and Jerry

B   Tom's claim will fail as Tom and Jerry failed to take reasonable care of themselves and others, as required by the H&S legislation so they are primarily to blame.

Activity 4: Bonny and Clive

C   Bonny is not guilty of bribery, Clive is. Bonny has provided what looks like legitimate corporate hospitality. Clive has tried to bribe a public official in order to manipulate his performance of a public duty.

Activity 5: Luigi and Mario

B and D

Luigi suspected Mario of money laundering so should have reported this to the money laundering officer within his firm. He compounds this mistake by tipping Mario off, putting a potential criminal prosecution at risk.

Activity 6: Data protection

A and D

These options are correct, B is incorrect as compensation will only be payable if Sarah can show a loss. C is incorrect as these records are exempt.

Activity 7: Whistleblowing

D   Options A, B and C are correct. D will not provide a defence; however, the seriousness of the matter is one of the factors considered in determining whether a disclosure made was reasonable in all the ci.

Test your learning

1   John works for Netco's information technology (IT) department. To save costs, Netco has outsourced John's department to Intco, an unrelated business which provides IT services to a number of businesses. John's continuity of service is protected by the Transfer of Undertaking rules.

True ☐
False ☐

2   The Health and Safety Commission, working though the Health and Safety Executive, oversees the working of the Health and Safety system in the UK.

True ☐
False ☐

3   The Bribery Act applies to companies and employees working in the UK only

True ☐
False ☐

4   Which of the following applies in the event of a valid whistleblowing?

A   The worker is entitled to keep his job
B   The employer is liable to a fine
C   The worker may claim damages
D   The employer must make a written apology to the worker

5   Which of the following is NOT an offence under the Proceeds of Crime Act which regulates money laundering?

A   Tipping off
B   Laundering
C   Dealing
D   Failure to report

6   Which of the following are principles of Data Protection as laid out by the Data Protection Act 1998? Tick all that apply.

Lawful processing   ☐
Accurate   ☐
Access   ☐
Compensation   ☐
Transfer outside Europe ☐
Junk mail   ☐

Dismissal and redundancy 15

Learning outcomes

Having studied this chapter you will be able to:

- Explain the distinction between unfair and wrongful dismissal and the consequences

Syllabus context

When an employment relationship is terminated, this may give rise to differing rights for employees and self-employed workers. It is crucial that you are able to distinguish between the types of dismissal, who is entitled to claim them and the remedies available.

A particular type of dismissal is redundancy, you will learn your rights and the statutory remedies available to people whose jobs effectively no longer exist.

Chapter overview

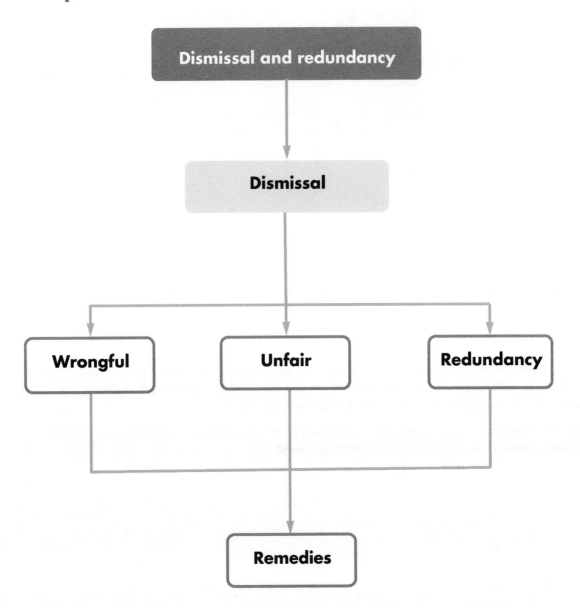

1 Ending the employment relationship

1.1 The employment relationship can end without a breach of contract in the following ways:

(a) Serving notice
(b) Payment in lieu of notice
(c) Expiry of a fixed term
(d) Mutual agreement
(e) Frustration.

1.2 Notice periods are typically agreed between the parties in the written contract of employment. There are, however, statutory minimum periods that apply.

Length of service	Minimum notice period
1 month – less than 2 years	At least 1 week
> 2 years	1 week for each continuous year worked
12 years or more	Minimum of 12 weeks

Key term

Dismissal refers to situations where the employer decides to terminate the employment relationship.

1.3 This also includes circumstances where the employer chooses not to renew a fixed term contract.

1.4 Other forms of dismissal that may constitute a breach of contract and give rise to a claim include:

(a) Summary dismissal
(b) Constructive dismissal
(c) Wrongful dismissal
(d) Unfair dismissal.

Summary dismissal

Key term

Summary dismissal occurs when the employee is 'sacked on the spot' eg without any notice.

1.5 This can only be justified by the employer where they are able to demonstrate that the employee has committed an act that equates to a conditional breach of contract, such as gross misconduct (see wrongful dismissal below). If this is not the case, then the employee has been wrongfully, and possibly unfairly dismissed.

Constructive dismissal

Constructive dismissal occurs when an employee, who has resigned, is able to prove they did so under duress from their employer, and as such, was therefore actually dismissed.

1.6 It is up to the employee to prove there was sufficiently unfair behaviour by the employer to constitute a material breach of contract. Case law examples include:

(a) Changing terms of the contract without consultation
(b) Making significant changes to the location of work at short notice
(c) Victimising or harassing staff.

Illustration 1

Brian got married to his long-term partner Freddie, and started wearing a wedding ring to work. Having kept his relationship quiet up to that point many, of Brian's colleagues asked about the ring and congratulated him on his recent nuptials. Brian's boss, John, made clear his disapproval then informed Brian that he was being immediately transferred to an office located 600 miles away, and would have to work night shifts, rather than his current 9am to 5pm working arrangements. To make matters worse, John tells Brian that when he transfers, his pay will fall 30% due to regional pay structures. Brian is very upset as his contract does not contain a mobility clause, and resigns in tears on the spot.

In these circumstances, Brian would be able to launch a claim with the Employment Tribunal for constructive dismissal. He appears to the victim of discrimination, and this, alongside the sudden and unlawful changes to his contract, will amount to a breach of contract on his employer's behalf, giving Brian the right to resign and claim he has, in fact, been constructively dismissed.

1.7 A successful claim for constructive dismissal gives the worker the right to launch an unfair dismissal claim.

1.8 Where an employee does not resign, they are deemed to have accepted the employers breach and consequently waived any rights.

Wrongful dismissal

Wrongful dismissal is a common law claim that can be made where an employee has been dismissed without justification, often when they have been denied their required notice period (see summary dismissal earlier).

1.9 This is commonly claimed by employees that do not qualify for unfair dismissal. Wrongful dismissal is comparable with a breach of contract.

1.10 The following have been held to be justification for dismissal:

(a) Wilful disobedience of a lawful order

(b) Misconduct, in connection with the business or outside it

(c) Dishonesty, where the employee is in a position of particular trust

(d) Incompetence or neglect

(e) Gross negligence

(f) Immorality, if likely to affect performance of duties or the reputation of the business

(g) Drunkenness, in aggravated circumstances such as when driving a vehicle.

Illustration 2

Dennis plays professional football for Foxes FC, and is aggrieved to hear that his contract will not be renewed at the end of the season. His performances in training deteriorate and he is dropped from the playing squad. Dennis demands that his contract is paid up in full, or else he will cease to attend training. Foxes FC refuse to acquiesce to his demands, since when Dennis has failed to attend training or matches.

At this point, Foxes FC would be within their rights to repudiate the contract of Dennis as his failure to attend training makes him unavailable for selection and would be a breach of a condition of the contract. Dennis could claim wrongful dismissal on the grounds that he has been sacked without paying up his contract. His claim would fail as his own conduct falls within the list of justifiable reasons for dismissal.

Unfair dismissal

Key term

Unfair dismissal is a statutory claim made by 'qualified' employees who have been 'unfairly dismissed'.

1.11 Any employee with at least two years continuous service has the right 'not to be unfairly dismissed'. Persons excluded from making claims include:

(a) Persons working outside of the UK
(b) Employees dismissed for taking part in unofficial strike action
(c) Excluded professions such as the police.

1.12 There are certain situations where the two year qualification is waived including dismissals relating to pregnancy, being denied a statutory right, or for raising concerns related to health and safety.

1.13 A dismissed employee must bring a claim to an Employment Tribunal (ET) within three months of dismissal. At this hearing, the employer must prove they had one of the following five fair reasons to dismiss the employee:

(a)   Capability or qualifications

(b)   Gross Misconduct

(c)   Redundancy

(d)   Statutory restrictions – such as a bus driver who receives a driving ban

(e)   Other substantial reasons – such as dismissing a temporary worker employed to cover another employee who has been suspended on medical grounds

1.14 There are certain circumstances where the employer cannot ever justify dismissal, and these are referred to as '**automatically unfair**' or '**inadmissible reasons**'. These include, but are not limited to:

(a)   Pregnancy
(b)   A spent conviction
(c)   Official trade union membership / activities
(d)   Seeking to maintain health and safety
(e)   Enforcing rights to the minimum wage / working time regulations.

1.15 When considering a, the tribunal will consider the behaviour of both parties, with particular regard as to whether they have acted 'reasonably'. In respect of the employer, they will be asked:

(a)   Did they apply the correct procedures?
(b)   Did they take all relevant circumstances into consideration?
(c)   What would any reasonable employer have done?

1.16 Key to reasonableness is often whether the employer has followed the ACAS Code of Practice on Disciplinary and Grievance Procedures. The code recommends the following stages:

(1)   Employer investigates to establish the facts

(2)   Employee is informed of the problem

(3)   Meeting held between the parties at which the employee can be accompanied

(4)   A decision is made

(5)   The employee has the right of appeal.

Activity 1: Dismissal

Required

Which of the following are examples of dismissal?

(i) An employee resigns following their employer's serious repudiatory breach of the employment contract

(ii) An employer terminates an employee's contract with notice

(iii) An employer fails to renew an employee's fixed term contract

(iv) An employee is offered garden leave

A (i), (iii) and (iv) only

B (i) and (ii) only

C (iii) only

D All of the above

Solution

---

2 Redundancy

2.1 As seen earlier, redundancy is a fair reason for dismissal. In fact, in cases of dismissal of any kind, there is a general presumption of redundancy. There are two statutory definitions of redundancy being:

(a) The employer has ceased, or intends to cease, to carry on in business for the purposes of the which the employee was employed, or in the place where the employee was employed

or

(b) That the requirements of that type of business for employees to carry out work of a particular kind, or in a particular place have ceased, or are expected to diminish or cease.

2.2 In order to make a redundancy claim, there are two qualification criteria that the employee must prove:

(a) That they were an employee

(b) Two years continuous employment have been served

2.3 Employees lose the right to claim redundancy if:

(a) They could have been dismissed for misconduct

(b) An offer to renew their contract is unreasonably refused

(c) A claim is made out of time – six months

(d) The employee leaves before being made redundant, having been notified of redundancy risk.

Illustration 3

Dolly is 57 and has worked in her local pub for many years as a barmaid. In an effort to make the bar more profitable, the landlord has decided to install disco and karaoke equipment, and has informed Dolly that she is being made redundant as the bar will need younger and more attractive bar staff, more in keeping with its new younger clientele.

Dolly could challenge her redundancy at tribunal as, in reality, there has been no actual change in the nature of the particular work done. In effect, Dolly has been wrongfully and unfairly dismissed for reasons of age discrimination.

Activity 2: Redundancy

Required

Which **two** of the following are circumstances where an employee will **not** be entitled to claim a redundancy payment?

(1) They could have been dismissed for misconduct before the redundancy notice
(2) Their claim is not made within three months of the redundancy notice   *6 mths*
(3) They are involved in strike action after the redundancy notice is served
(4) They unreasonably refuse a renewal to their contract

A   1 and 3
B   1 and 4
C   2 and 3
D   2 and 4

Solution

---

3   Remedies

3.1 As discussed earlier wrongful dismissal is essentially a breach of contract. As such the employee may make a claim for damages in either:

(a) Employment tribunal for claims up to £25,000
(b) County or High Court for claims over £25,000.

3.2 An unfair dismissal claim is a statutory claim so is therefore brought before an employment tribunal. Any subsequent appeal may be heard by an Employment Appeals Tribunal (EAT). The tribunal has the power to award the following types of remedies:

(a) Reinstatement – being restored to your old position

(b) Re-engagement – being re-engaged in a different, but comparable position

(c) Compensation – there are three elements to an award:

- Basic award, linked to age and length of service

- Compensatory award, for loss of wages may be awarded in addition to the basic award at the discretion of the tribunal

- Additional award, of up to 52 weeks' pay may be granted in cases of sex or race discrimination.

3.3 The basic award is calculated in the same way as for redundancy, as shown below. This award, along with the compensatory award, are capped at statutory maximum levels that are reviewed annually.

3.4 In the event that the employer is found to have acted unreasonably, for instance by failing to follow the ACAS code, any awards can be increased by up to 25%. Similarly, if the employee fails to act reasonably, their award can be reduced by 25%.

3.5 Dismissal by way of redundancy gives rise to the basic claim as follows:

Age	Entitlement (weeks' pay)
18-21	½
22-40	1
41+	1½

3.6 The basic award is limited to a maximum 20 years, and assumes a maximum weekly wage capped at an amount reviewed annually.

Activity 3: Unfair dismissal

Required

the compensatory award element .. (handwritten)

Which of the following statements regarding compensation for unfair dismissal is **not** correct?

- A   Compensation may be reduced if it is just and equitable to do so
- B   Compensation may be reduced if it is greater than lost earnings
- C   Compensation may be reduced if the employee contributed to their own dismissal
- D   Compensation may be reduced if the employee unreasonably refused an offer of reinstatement

Solution

Chapter summary

- Where employment is **terminated** by **notice,** the period given must not be less than the statutory minimum.

- If an employee is dismissed with **shorter notice** than the statutory or contractual requirements, or **without notice** when **summary dismissal** is unjustified, the employer can be sued for **wrongful dismissal**.

- Certain employees have a right not to be **unfairly dismissed**. Breach of that right allows an employee to claim **compensation** from a **tribunal**. To claim for unfair dismissal, the employee must satisfy **certain criteria**.

- Dismissal must be justified if it related to the employee's **capability** or **qualifications**, the employee's **conduct**, **redundancy**, **legal prohibition** or restriction on the employee's continued employment or some other substantial reason. Some reasons for dismissal are automatically fair or unfair.

- Even where the reason for dismissal is justified or automatically fair, the tribunal must also decide whether the **employer acted reasonably** in the circumstances.

- Remedies for unfair dismissal include:

  - **Reinstatement**
  - **Re-engagement**
  - **Compensation**.

- **Constructive dismissal:** occurs when an employee, who has resigned, is able to prove they did so under duress from their employer, and as such, was therefore actually dismissed.

- **Dismissal:** refers to situations where the employer decides to terminate the employment relationship.

- **Summary dismissal:** occurs when the employee is 'sacked on the spot' eg without any notice.

- **Unfair dismissal:** is a statutory claim made by 'qualified' employees who have been 'unfairly dismissed'.

- **Wrongful dismissal:** is a common law claim that can be made where an employee has been dismissed without justification, often when they have been denied their required notice period (see summary dismissal earlier).

Activity answers

Activity 1: Dismissal

D   All of the options are examples of dismissal eg where the employer decides to terminate the employment relationship.

Activity 2: Redundancy

B   Employees who were or could have been dismissed before the redundancy notice cannot claim a redundancy payment. An employee who unreasonably refuses a renewal to their contract cannot claim a redundancy payment. A claim can be made within six months and those involved in strike action after the redundancy notice can claim a redundancy payment.

Activity 3: Unfair dismissal

B   Compensation for unfair dismissal is a statutory concept, not just based on common law principles relating to breach of contract. It will not be reduced just because it may exceed lost earnings. The other options are circumstances where an award may be reduced.

1   Rick was employed by Chingtow Ltd, earning a salary of £24,000 pa and entitled to three months' notice from his employer. However, he was wrongfully dismissed with one month's notice. How much will the court award him as compensation?

A   £2,000
B   £4,000
C   £6,000
D   £8,000

2   The usual remedy for wrongful dismissal is

A   Reinstatement
B   Damages
C   Redundancy pay
D   Re-engagement

3   Unfavourable treatment of a woman purely due to her pregnancy is classed as sex discrimination.

True ☐
False ☐

4   **Fill in the blanks** below, using the words in the box.

To claim (1) .... for unfair dismissal, three issues have to be considered.

- The employee must show that he is a (2) .... employee and that he has been (3) ....

- The (4) .... must explain the (5) .... for dismissal

- Application has to be made to the (6) .... within (7) .... months of the dismissal

• qualifying	• dismissed	• employer
• reason	• three	• compensation
• employment tribunal		

5   Which of the following is an automatically unfair reason for dismissal?

A   Gross misconduct
B   Taking unofficial strike action
C   Breaching health and safety
D   Enforcing rights to a maximum working week

Legal personality 16

Learning outcomes

Having studied this chapter you will be able to:

- Describe the essential characteristics of the different forms of business organisations and the implications of corporate personality

- Explain the main advantages and disadvantages of carrying on business through the medium of a company limited by shares

- Explain the ability of a company to contract

Syllabus context

When starting a business, one of the most important decisions to make will be the choice of trading vehicle. Aside from the tax status (which is not examinable in this paper) the proprietor will need to balance the risk of personal liability associated with a traditional simple partnership against the onerous disclosure and administrative features of an LLP or limited company.

Chapter overview

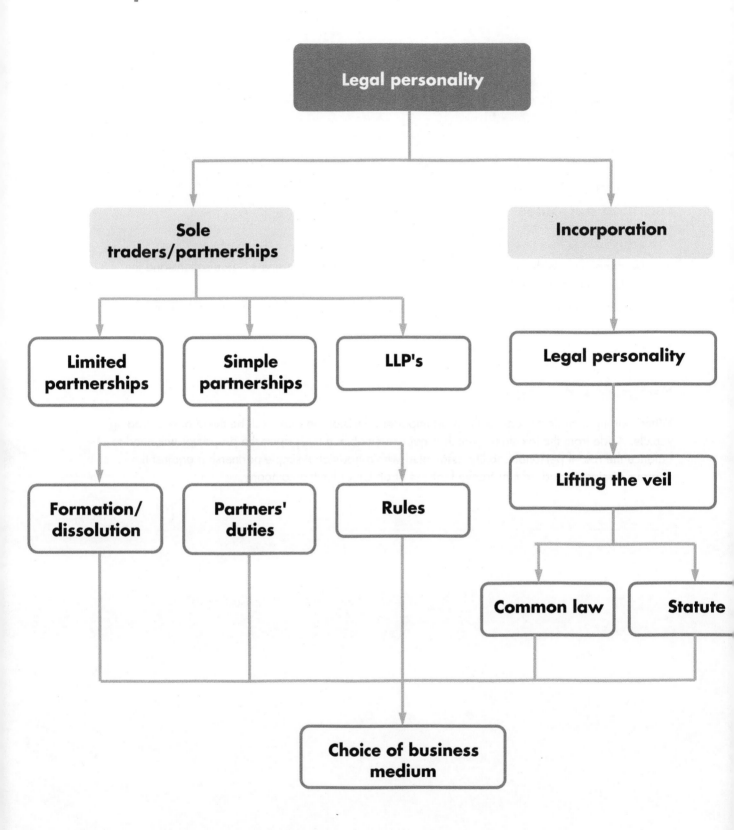

1 Sole tradership / Standard partnership

1.1 **Standard partnerships** are those governed by the **Partnership Act 1890** (PA 1890). This is defined by the Act as being:

Key term

| **Partnership** | The relationship that subsists between persons carrying on a business in common with a view to profit. |

1.2 The importance of this definition is that any trading relationship that fits this description will be treated by the courts as a partnership, irrespective of the way it is classified by its owners. As such, it is clear that the standard partnership is **not a separate legal entity** and its partners therefore have **full personal liability** for the debts of the partnership.

1.3 These partnerships may be governed by a private **partnership agreement** drawn up between the partners themselves. Any aspect of the partnership not covered by such an agreement, will be governed by the PA 1890. Some of the main rights accruing to partners per the PA 1890 are to:

    (a)   Share equally in the capital and profits of the business
    (b)   Be indemnified by the firm for any liabilities
    (c)   Take part in the management of the business
    (d)   Have access to the firm's books
    (e)   Prevent admission of a new partner or a change in partnership nature.

1.4 There are no specific requirements to create a standard partnership. Indeed where a business relationship is deemed by the courts to fit the definition given in section 1.1 the courts will imply the formation of a standard partnership.

1.5 Standard partnerships will be **dissolved** in many ways, including the following:

    (a)   Expiry of a fixed period for which the partnership was formed
    (b)   Completion of the express purpose for which the partnership was formed
    (c)   Activity of the partnership becomes illegal
    (d)   Partner gives notice to leave (subject to PA 1890)
    (e)   Death or bankruptcy of a partner (subject to PA 1890).

Illustration 1

Alison, Ben, Caroline and David begin working together, having previously been trading as independent accountants. Their motivation to work together was that they felt they could share costs and win business from larger clients by joining forces. Despite not agreeing on a partnership agreement document and naming their business 'ABCD' for three months the partnership in fact came into being the moment they started trading together per the definition in the PA 1890.

Three years later Caroline decides to change career and become an interior designer. In her place, Alison, Ben and David invite Emily to join the partnership. As far as third parties are concerned, a partnership offering accountancy services still exists. In law however the old partnership (ABCD) has been dissolved, and a new partnership (ABDE) has replaced it.

Partners' duties

1.6 The relationship between the partners is a **fiduciary** one of '**utmost good faith**'. In addition to these general fiduciary duties there are specific **statutory duties**:

(a) The duty **to disclose** – all partners must render true accounts and full information in matters relating to the partnership

(b) The duty **to account** – partners must account for all benefits obtained from any transaction related to the partnership

(c) The duty **not to compete** – a partner who competes against the partnership without consent will be liable for all such profits made.

Partnership property

1.7 Property can either be the property of an individual partner, or owned by the partnership as a whole, and in the case of the latter is known as **partnership property**. It is important to distinguish the nature of ownership for the following reasons:

(a) Partnership property must be used exclusively for partnership business

(b) Partnership property is used to pay partners' debts upon dissolution

(c) The increase in value of property passes to the owner, either the partnership or the individual, depending on the nature of its ownership.

Partners' authority

1.8 Partners are deemed to be agents of the firm, and as such have **implied actual authority** to bind the firm in ordinary trading transactions. However, the partnership agreement can be used to expressly widen or restrict these powers.

1.9 The power of partners to bind the partnership in contract with third parties is illustrated below:

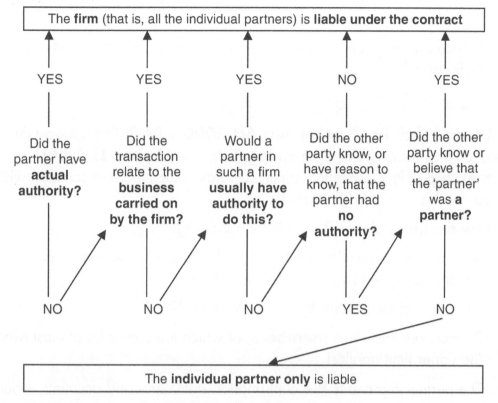

1.10 As well as personal liability for the trading debts of the firm, the partners may also be liable for torts committed by other partners. In such cases, the partners are said to be **joint and severally liable**, allowing the claimant to sue either the partner responsible or the firm. Where an individual is sued, they may claim contributions from the other partners in line with the profit sharing agreement.

1.11 A partner's liability usually extends to the periods for which they were actually a partner of the firm. As such, partners who join or leave would not expect to be liable for torts committed in the periods before they joined or left.

1.12 In such circumstances however, where it can be proved that an individual was being **held out** as a partner at the time of the tort, liability will be extended to them. It is important, therefore, that new/retiring partners advertise widely using the *London Gazette* and that the partnership documents the effective date of their appointment/retirement.

2 Limited partnerships

2.1 An increasingly rare business form is the Limited Partnership, as defined by the **Limited Partnership Act 1907** (LPA 1907).

2.2 This Act allowed for the creation of a trading entity that enabled some of its partners to limit their liability in the event of a liquidation, subject to the following restrictions.

(a) The partnership must be registered with the Companies Registry

(b)   One or more of the partners must retain full, unlimited liability

(c)   Partners with limited liability may not take part in the management of the business, and cannot usually bind the business in contract

(d)   Limited partners cannot, in the ordinary course of business, withdraw their capital.

3   Limited liability partnerships

3.1   The **Limited Liability Partnership Act 2000** (LLPA 2000) allowed the formation of a new type of legal trading entity, the **Limited Liability Partnership** (LLP). Despite the name, LLPs have much more in common with companies than standard partnerships.

3.2   The **key features** of an LLP include the following:

(a)   Must be registered with the Registrar of Companies, with formation documents signed by at least two members

(b)   The name of the partnership must end with LLP

(c)   Partners are known as **members**, of which there must be at least two (no upper limit applies)

(d)   The partnership **must file** confirmation statements and accounts; where applicable, an audit is also required

(e)   The LLP is a **separate legal entity** with all of the associated features this entails

(f)   **Members are agents** of the LLP, and can bind in the same way as partners in a standard partnership

(g)   **Members' liability is limited** to an amount stated in the partnership document (no lower limit exists)

(h)   A **designated member**(s) is (are) responsible for administration and filing

(i)   The LLP is not subject to **corporation tax**; the members therefore enjoy the same taxable status as partners of a standard partnership.

Activity 1: Partnerships

Barry and Paul begin working together to create a hair restoration cream. Most of the capital was provided by Wendy, who leaves Barry and Paul to run the business as they see fit. Wendy presented Barry and Paul with some paperwork, which they duly signed, and having filed this with the relevant authorities, they began work in their laboratory.

Having spent two years formulating a cream, they were horrified that, during the human testing a number of the volunteers experience accelerated hair loss and irritable bowels. Several of the volunteers sought legal advice and Barry and Paul are shocked to discover that they alone are fully liable for the full value of the legal claims.

Required

What type of business relationship has been formed?

A   Traditional partnership   ✓ *no paperwork to file w. authorities*
B   Limited company
C   Limited liability partnership   ] – *co/ LLP wld be liab*
Ⓓ   Limited partnership

Solution   ↳ *still expect W to have limited liab?*

---

4   Incorporation

4.1   A company is an example of an **incorporated trading entity**.

Key term

> The term '**incorporation**' means than an entity has been created in its own right and is thus known as a '**corporation**', and is therefore separated in law from its owners.

Standard partnerships and sole traders do not require such formal creation, and as such, are not corporations.

4.2   In order to confer limited liability upon its members, a company or LLP requires incorporation. However, it is important to appreciate that incorporation itself does not guarantee limited liability in every circumstance, as discussed below in Section 6.

Illustration 2

Some official positions are what is known as Corporations Sole. Examples of this would include the Mayor of London, the Prime Minister and the Archbishop of Canterbury.

The effect of this is that if the person holding any of these offices is negligent, then it is the corporation that gets sued, not the individual office holder.

5 Legal personality

5.1 The concept of separate legal personality was permitted to be applied to private companies in the case of *Salomon v Salomon & Co* **(1)**. In essence it was established that the members of a company were separate legal persons to the company itself, separated by the '**veil of incorporation**' as seen below:

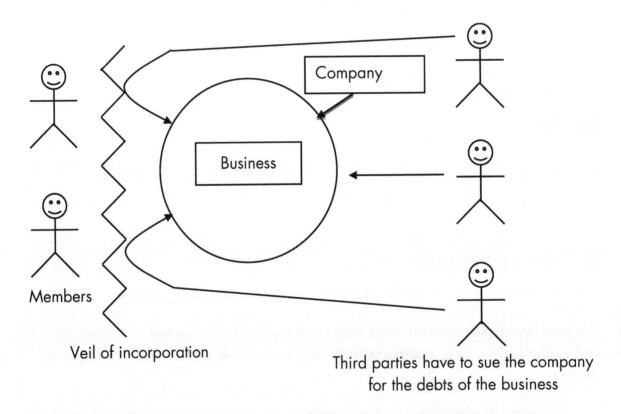

Members

Veil of incorporation

Third parties have to sue the company
for the debts of the business

5.2 The consequences of separate legal personality for the company are as follows:

(a) Members' liability is limited

(b) Perpetual succession arises as the company will need to be formally wound up

(c) The company itself can own property

(d) The company can sue, and be sued in its own name

(e) The company can contract in its own name, as defined by its Articles

Activity 2: Tom

Required

Tom has transferred his business to Tom Ltd, a company limited by shares. Which of the following statements is correct?

A   Tom Ltd is fully liable for all debts and liabilities of the business incurred after the date of transfer.

B   Tom is fully liable for all debts and liabilities of the business incurred after the date of transfer.

C   Tom and Tom Ltd are jointly liable for all debts and liabilities of the business incurred after the date of transfer.

D   Tom Ltd and its shareholders are fully liable for all debts and liabilities incurred after the date of transfer.

Solution

---

6 Lifting the veil

6.1   It has been recognised that, in a number of circumstances, the operation of the veil of incorporation would allow people to evade their legal obligations, or use companies to commit frauds. As such, there are common law and statutory exceptions to the general rule in *Salomon v Salomon*. Under these exceptions, the veil is lifted, meaning that the members or directors of a company can be held personally liable for the debts of the company.

6.2   The **common law** exceptions are as follows:

  (a)   Where a company is being used **to evade legal duties** – *Gilford Motor Co v Horne* **(2)**

  (b)   To recognise the **alien enemy character** of a company – *Daimler Co Ltd v Continental Tyre and Rubber Co (GB) Ltd* **(3)**

  (c)   To identify the **controlling mind** of a company in cases of corporate manslaughter – *R v OLL Ltd* **(4)**

  (d)   Recognising **the breakdown of a quasi-partnership** relationship – *Ebrahimi v Westborne Galleries* **(5)**

  (e)   Where a group of companies is operating as '**a single economic entity**' – *DHN v Tower Hamlets* **(6)**. (Note this exception to the general rule for group companies per *Adams v Cape Industries* **(7)**.)

Illustration 3

Lifting the veil of incorporation is permitted when the person or persons are using the incorporation of a company to evade or deliberately frustrate a legal obligation or liability. Such an occasion occurred in the case of Petrodel Resources Ltd and Others v Prest, which was heard in the Supreme Court.

Mr Michael Prest was born in Nigeria and Mrs Yasmin Prest was born in England; both had dual Nigerian and English nationality. They were married in 1993 and lived in England, although the husband was resident in Monaco from 2001. There was also a second home in Nevis. The husband owned and controlled a group of oil trading companies, two of which owned seven residential properties in London. In the divorce proceedings, Mrs Prest applied for a lump sum of £30m. She also applied for a declaration that the properties were held by the companies on trust for the husband or that he was beneficially entitled to them. Mr Prest, who was resident outside the court's jurisdiction, offered a package worth a little over £2m. The Family Division judge found that the husband had attempted to conceal the value of his assets, estimated at £37.5m, and that his purpose in vesting the legal interest in the properties was wealth protection and avoidance of tax. The judge held that the properties were effectively his assets in spite of having been owned by the companies. This was a rare decision, as it contradicted the decision in *Salomon v Salomon* which established the principle of separate corporate identity.

6.3 **Statute** provides for the lifting of the veil in the following circumstances:

   (a) Failing to correctly disclose the company's full name on company documents

   (b) Fraudulent trading – continuing to trade a company with intent to defraud creditors, or any other fraudulent purpose

   (c) Wrongful trading – continuing to trade an insolvent company with no intent proven.

Activity 3: Lifting the veil

Required

In which TWO of the following circumstances may the veil of incorporation NOT be lifted?

(1) To allow directors of insolvent companies to be found liable for the debts of the company

(2) To treat a group company as a single economic entity

(3) To allow an auditor access to company records _____ *??*

(4) To allow a private company to re-register as a public company. _ *??*

A   1 and 2
B   1 and 3
C   2 and 3
D   3 and 4

Solution

7 Choice of business medium

7.1 When considering whether or not to trade via an incorporated or unincorporated trading entity it is essential to understand the advantages of both mediums.

(a) **Incorporated**:

- Limited liability for members
- Perpetual succession
- Transferability of interest
- Company owns its own assets
- Company may sue/be sued
- Ease of borrowing – floating charges
- No limit on number of members

(b) **Unincorporated**:

- Less formality upon inception/running the business
- Less publicity – no filing of accounts
- Less expensive – no audit requirement
- No restrictions on the withdrawal of capital

- In a **sole tradership**, there is **no legal distinction** between the individual and the business.

- Partnership is defined as '**the relationship which subsists between persons carrying on a business in common with a view of profit**'. A partnership is not a separate legal person distinct from its members, it is merely a 'relation' between persons. Each partner (there must be at least two) is **personally liable** for all the debts of the firm.

- Partnerships can be formed very **informally**, but there may be complex formalities to ensure clarity.

- Partnerships may be **terminated** by, passing of **time**, termination of the underlying venture, **death** or **bankruptcy** of a partner, **illegality**, **notice**, **agreement** or by **order** of the court.

- The **authority** of partners to bind each other in contract is based on the principles of **agency**.

- Partners are **jointly liable** for all partnership debts that result from contracts that the partners have made which bind the firm.

- A **limited liability partnership** formed under the **2000 Act** combines the features of a traditional partnership with the limited liability and creation of a legal personality more usually associated with limited companies.

- A company has a **legal personality** separate from its owners (known as members). It is a formal arrangement, surrounded by formality and publicity, but its chief advantage is that members' liability for the company's debts is typically limited.

- The fact that a **company's members** – not the company itself – hav**e limited liability** for its debts protects the members from the company's creditors and ultimately, from the full risk of business failure.

- The case of **Salomon v Salomon & Co Ltd** clearly demonstrates the separate legal personality of companies and is of great significance to any study of company law.

- Incorporation **'veils'** members from outsiders' view but this veil may be lifted in some circumstances, so creditors and others can seek redress directly from members. The **veil may be lifted**: by **statute** to enforce the law; to prevent the **evasion of obligations**; and in certain situations where companies trade as a group.

Keywords

- The term **'incorporation'** means than an entity has been created in its own right and is thus known as a 'corporation', and is therefore separated in law from its owners.

- **Partnership:** The relationship that subsists between persons carrying on a business in common with a view to profit.

Activity 1: Partnerships

D   Limited partnership – The scenario indicates that Wendy is a silent investor who merely provides capital and does not interfere in the running of the business. This allows her to escape the personal liability that Barry and Paul have.

Activity 2: Tom

A   The company has a separate legal identity - *Salomon v Salomon & Co.*

Activity 3: Lifting the veil

D   The veil has been lifted where fraudulent / wrongful trading was proven, or, where a company has been acting as a single economic entity, but not for examples 3 and 4 .

Test your learning

1   Which one of the following statements about traditional (unlimited) partnerships is **incorrect**?

   A   In England a partnership has no existence distinct from the partners
   B   A partnership must have a written partnership agreement
   C   A partnership is subject to the Partnership Act
   D   Each partner is an agent of the firm.

2   Under which circumstance would a member of a limited company have to contribute funds on winding up?

   A   Where there is not enough cash to pay the creditors

   B   Where they have an outstanding amount from when they originally purchased their shares

   C   To allow the company to repurchase debentures it issued

   D   Where the company is a community interest company and the funds are required to complete a community project

3   A consequence of the principle of corporate personality is that company debts must be paid out of company assets.

   True   ☐
   False ☐

4   Which of the following describes how a traditional (unlimited) partnership is taxed?

   A   The partnership pays tax on its profits
   B   The partners are taxed through the PAYE system
   C   The partners receive dividends on which they pay income tax
   D   Partners extract drawings on which they are subject to income tax

5   Businesses in the form of sole traders are legally distinct from their owners.

   True   ☐
   False ☐

1 Salomon v Salomon and Co

S transferred his business as a sole trader into a company legally incorporated with the correct number of shareholders. Sale of assets to the company meant S was owed money by S and Co, which was secured by a debenture. On subsequent liquidation, this took priority over unsecured trade creditors who argued it was invalid as the creditor – S – and the debtor – S and Co – were technically one and the same. It was held that this was incorrect. The company, being validly constituted, was a separate legal entity to S and the debt was upheld.

2 Gilford Motor Co v Horne

H was a car salesman, and left G. His contract stated that he wasn't allowed to sell to G's customers for a period after leaving. H set up a company which then approached his former customers; H argued that firstly his company was approaching the customers, not him; and secondly, if there was wrongdoing, his company was liable and not him. The courts held that the company was a sham, and granted an injunction against his company as well as him.

3 Daimler Co Ltd v Continental Tyre and Rubber Co (GB) Ltd

C sued D for debts owing. C was a UK company; however all shareholders but one were German. D argued that they should not pay the debt to German individuals to prevent money going towards Germany's war effort. The court held that C was German.

4 R v OLL Ltd

On 8 December 1994, OLL Ltd became the first company in English legal history to be convicted of corporate manslaughter. Peter Kite, 45, its managing director, also became the first director to be given an immediate custodial sentence for a manslaughter conviction arising from the operation of a business. Both defendants were found guilty on four counts of manslaughter arising from the death of four teenagers who drowned off Lyme Regis while on a canoe trip, on 22 March 1993, organised by the defendant, OLL Ltd.

Mr Kite was sentenced to three years' imprisonment; the company was fined £60,000. An appalling catalogue of errors led to the deaths of the four teenagers who drowned having been in the sea for over four hours after their canoes capsized. According to those familiar with canoeing, the trip should never have taken place. Prior to the trip, the teenagers had received only one hour of tuition in a swimming pool by unqualified staff.

The weather forecast on the day of the trip had not been checked properly, distress flares were not provided by the company, and the only safety equipment possessed by the instructors was a whistle. The students' canoes did not have 'spray decks' to keep out water. Nine months before the disaster, two instructors had left the company because they were not satisfied with its safety policy. One wrote a letter to the managing director, Mr Kite, urging him to take a 'careful look' at safety, otherwise he might find himself explaining 'why someone's son or daughter will not be coming home'.

5 Ebrahimi v Westborne Galleries

E and friend N set up a gallery in Holland Park. Initially, it was a partnership and then N suggested setting up a Ltd Co. to attain limited liability. Shares were allocated on a 50/50 basis with equal management rights.

N then introduced his son to the company, effectively reducing E's shares to 49%. N and his son passed an ordinary resolution, sacking E as a director and then paid bonuses to the directors and declared a nil dividend. E applied to the courts for just and equitable winding up. It was held that the company was, in legal effect, a partnership based on a relationship of mutual trust and confidence which had clearly broken down. The court wound the company up.

6 DHN Food Distributors v Tower Hamlets LBC

The veil was lifted to recognise that subsidiaries of a company which were in occupation of premises that were the subject of a compulsory purchase order, and, were one and the same as the holding company. As a result, the money could be paid to the holding company because the group of companies was viewed as 'one economic entity'.

This case was subsequently held to be applicable only in specific circumstances. The general rule is the one followed in *Adams v Cape Industries* below.

7 Adams v Cape Industries

Cape, an English company, was head of a group including wholly owned subsidiaries.

In the United States, claimants had been awarded damages for asbestosis against a marketing company NAAC, a subsidiary of Cape.

The Court of Appeal held that the judgement could not be enforced against Cape, as the subsidiary was to be treated as a 'separate legal entity with all the rights and liabilities which would normally attach to separate legal entities...'

Company formation 17

Having studied this chapter you will be able to:

- Explain the differences between public and private companies
- Explain the ability of a company to contract

Syllabus context

Forming a company is a relatively bureaucratic process. In this chapter you will learn the steps involved in incorporating a company; but also how these can be circumvented by simply purchasing a company already formed by someone else (an off-the-shelf company). Once a company is formed more bureaucracy arises in terms of the keeping and maintaining so called 'statutory books'.

Chapter overview

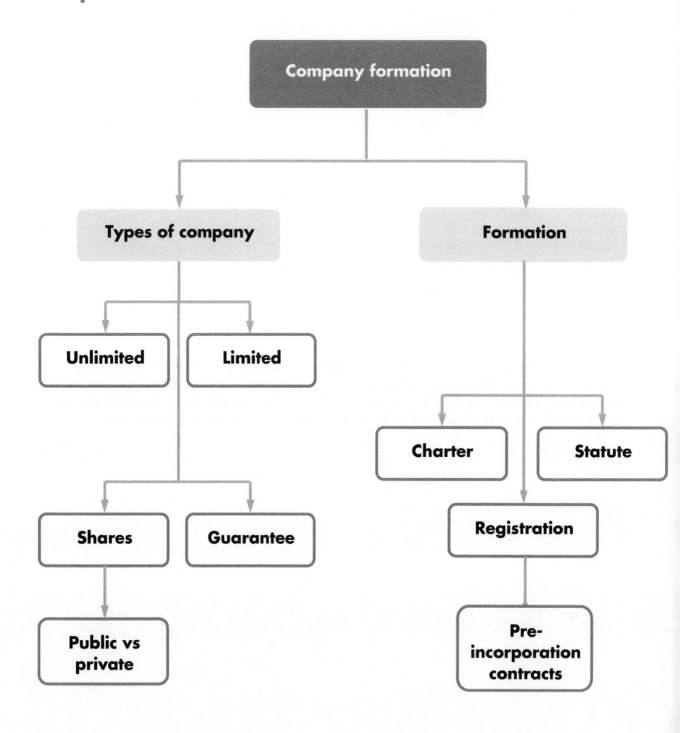

1 Types of company

1.1

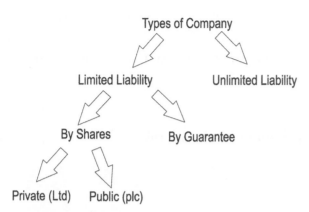

Types of Company
- Limited Liability
- Unlimited Liability

Limited Liability
- By Shares
- By Guarantee

By Shares
- Private (Ltd)
- Public (plc)

1.2 **Unlimited companies** share all the features of separate legal personality as limited companies, save for the limited liability afforded to its members. In return however, they do not have to file their accounts nor make them available for public inspection.

1.3 **Companies limited by guarantee** are those that limit the liability of its members to an agreed amount, often being a nominal figure for the protection of the guarantor(s). Certain non-trading entities such as charities and educational establishments choose to adopt this company form as it allows them to drop the suffix 'Ltd' from some the company documents.

1.4 **Private limited companies** account for >99% of all registered companies in the UK. These are companies that limit the liability of their members to the amount unpaid on their share capital.

1.5 **Public limited companies** are similar to private limited companies in that they limit the liability of their members via the use of shares. However, in a plc, the shares or debentures in issue **may be advertised for sale** to the general public, and a stock market listing may be applied for. It is important to note however, that not all plcs are listed on a stock market.

1.6 The main differences between Ltd and Plc companies are summarised below.

Features	Ltd	plc
Minimum number of directors	1	2
Minimum number of members	1	1
Minimum share capital	One share	£50,000
Advertise shares/debentures to public	No	Yes
Time to hold accounting records	3 years	6 years
Annual general meeting	Optional	Compulsory
Company secretary	Optional	Compulsory
File accounts after year-end	9 months	6 months

Activity 1: Marvin

Marvin is trying to find a cure for cancer, but given the risks involved, does not want to expose himself to the monetary risks of financial failure. His business will largely be funded by charitable donations, and will reinvest any annual surpluses into research.

Required

Which of the following business forms should Marvin adopt?

A   Public limited company
B   Company limited by guarantee
C   Unlimited liability company
D   Sole tradership

Solution

2   Formation

2.1   In order to form a company in the UK, the following documents must be lodged with the Registrar of Companies House in either Cardiff or Edinburgh; this may be done via an **online submission** or hard copy.

Document	Description
Memorandum of Association	Historic record of initial subscribers
Application for registration	Name, address, members' liability & company type
Section 9 documents	Share capital and initial shareholdings
Statement of compliance	Statutory declaration of compliance
£20	Registration fee

Section 9 Documents

2.2   Where a company is formed to be limited by shares, the following information must be provided:

(a)   The total number of shares (minimum of one) taken by the subscribers
(b)   The aggregate nominal value of those shares
(c)   For each separate class of share, their rights and aggregate values
(d)   The amounts paid up on each class of share.

2.3 Additionally, all companies must provide residential and service addresses for each natural director and secretary as well as the company's postal address.

2.4 Should a company wish to draft its own articles (see Chapter 18) then these will also need to be submitted.

Public companies

2.5 In order to **form a plc,** there is an additional requirement to apply for a **trading certificate** which requires submission of the following evidence.

   (a) Allotted share capital is at least £50,000

   (b) At least one quarter of the nominal value of the allotted share capital has been paid up (minimum £12,500)

   (c) Details of promoter's expenses

   (d) A statement of compliance in respect of payment of nominal values and share premium.

2.6 The consequences of a plc trading without the necessary documentation are that any transactions are valid; however, the company and its directors are punishable by a fine. After 12 months, the company may be compulsorily wound up; and the veil of incorporation lifted.

Certificate of incorporation

2.7 Once all of the documentation has been lodged, the registrar will issue a **certificate of incorporation**, which is final and conclusive proof of the effective birth date of the company, before which it may not trade – *Jubilee Cotton Mills v Lewis (1)*. Additionally, the Registrar will advertise the formation in the *Gazette*.

2.8 In addition to incorporating companies by **registration**, as detailed above, companies can be incorporated by:

   (a) **Royal Charter** – the BBC
   (b) **Statute** – railway and coal companies in the Industrial Age.

2.9 Alternatively, a company can be purchased '**off-the-shelf**', with the following advantages.

   (a) **Speed** – registration may take up to two weeks
   (b) **Cost** – a pre-registered company may cost as little as £30 to buy
   (c) **Administration** – all forms are completed by the formation dealer.

Pre-incorporation contracts

Key term

> Where contract are agreed before a company has been officially formed difficulties may arise with what are known as **pre-incorporation contracts**.

2.10 In order to avoid liability under these contracts the person who signed the contract, usually referred to as the promoter can:

(a) Attempt to **novate** the contract

(b) Form such contracts in **draft**

(c) Purchase a company '**off the shelf**'

Activity 2: Rupert

Required

Rupert decides that he will set up his own business providing pharmaceutical supplies direct to patients. Rupert's concern about getting new business means he wants to trade as soon as the company is set up. When will this be?

A   The day he receives the Certificate of Incorporation from the Registrar of Companies

B   At any time after the date that the Registrar of Companies signs the Certificate of Incorporation as his signature is conclusive evidence of the company's legal existence

C   At any time after the date on the Certificate of Incorporation as this is conclusive evidence of the company's legal existence

D   The day the Registrar of Companies receives and approves the application to register the company

Solution

3 Statutory books

3.1 The following registers must be kept by the company, though per the Companies Act 2006 allows for many of them to be stored electronically as long as soft copies can be generated:

Type
Register of **members**
Register of **people with significant control (PSC)**
Records of **directors** (and **secretaries**)
Register of **directors' residential addresses**
Records of **directors' service contracts** and indemnities
Records of **resolutions** and **meetings** of the company
Register of **debenture holders**
Register of disclosed **interests in shares** (public Co's only)
Register of **members**

3.2 A company must submit the following annually to the Registrar:

(a) Accounts within six or nine months of year end for plc's and Ltd companies respectively

(b) An annual confirmation statement – keeping the registrar informed about changes to the company such as changes to membership and share capital etc.

- Most companies are those incorporated under the Companies Act. However there are other types of company such as **corporations sole**, **chartered corporations**, **statutory corporations** and **community interest companies**.

- A company may be **private** or **public**. Only the latter may offer its shares to the public.

- To trade a public company must hold a Registrar's **trading certificate** having met the requirements, including **minimum capital of £50,000**.

- The main **differences** between **public** and **private** companies relate to: capital; dealings in shares, accounts, commencement of business; general meetings; names; identification; and disclosure requirements.

- **Pre-incorporation contracts** cannot be ratified by the company. A new contract on the same terms must be created.

- A company is formed and registered under the Companies Act 2006 when it is issued with a **Certificate of Incorporation** by the Registrar, after submission to the Registrar of a number of documents and a fee.

- Buying a company **'off-the-shelf'** avoids the administrative burden of registering a company.

- To trade or borrow, a public company needs a **trading certificate**. Private companies may commence business on registration.

- The price of limited liability is **greater public accountability** is via the Companies Registry, registers, the **London Gazette** and company letterheads.

- A company must keep **registers** of certain aspects of its constitution, including the registers of **members**, **charges** and **directors**.

- Companies must keep sufficient **accounting records** to explain the company's transactions and its financial position; in other words, so a profit and loss account and balance sheet can be prepared.

- A registered company must **prepare annual accounts** showing a true and fair view, lay them and various reports before members, and **file** them with the **Registrar** following directors' approval.

- Every company must make an **annual confirmation statement** to the Registrar.

Keywords

- Where contract are agreed before a company has been officially formed difficulties may arise with what are known as **pre-incorporation contracts**.

Activity 1: Marvin

B   Marvin is keen to avoid personal liability so needs a limited liability company. As a charitable/research company, he would benefit from being able to drop the word 'Ltd' from most of the company's paperwork, making it easier to solicit donations as this removes the inference of a profit motive.

Activity 2: Rupert

C   The date on the Certificate of Incorporation is final and conclusive evidence per *Jubilee Cotton Mills v Lewis*.

Test your learning

1   Which **two** of the following statements about private companies are true?

A private company is:

A   Defined as any company that is not a public company

B   One that sells its shares on the junior stock market known as the Alternative Investment Market and on the Stock Exchange

C   One that must have at least one director with unlimited liability

D   A significant form of business organisation in areas of the economy that do not require large amounts of capital

2   If a public company does business or borrows before obtaining a trading certificate from the Registrar, the transaction is:

A   Invalid, and the third party cannot recover any loss

B   Invalid, but the third party may recover any loss from the directors

C   Valid, and the directors are punishable by a fine

D   Valid, but the third party can sue the directors for further damages

3   A company can confirm a pre-incorporation contract by performing it or obtaining benefits from it.

True   ☐

False   ☐

4   A public company must appoint a company secretary.

True   ☐

False   ☐

5   Wooddan Ltd was registered on 6th March 20X7 by a business which specialises in setting up and selling 'off-the-shelf' companies. On 7th June 20X8, Woodan Ltd is brought by a promoter, Niall, who is setting up a new business. As part of setting up the business, Niall entered into a contract to lease some office space. This contract was signed on 4th April 20X7. Niall would like Woodan Ltd to ratify the contract for the lease so he is no longer liable on it.

Which of the following describes the legal position?

A   Wooddan Ltd cannot ratify the contract as Niall did not own the company when the lease was entered into

B   Woodan Ltd can ratify the contract as it existed when the contract was entered into

C   Wooddan Ltd cannot ratify the contract because it only existed as an off-the-shelf company when the contract was signed and as such, could not be party to it

D   Wooddan Ltd can ratify the contract, providing the company which set it up agrees

Case summaries

1 Jubilee Cotton Mills v Lewis

The date on a company's certificate of incorporation is conclusive evidence of the company's existence.

A company's constitution

18

Learning outcomes

Having studied this chapter you will be able to:

- Explain the purpose and legal status of the articles of association

Syllabus context

The articles of a company are a vital document that regulates its internal affairs. Given that the articles operate as the company's internal rulebook the Companies Act 2006 (CA 06) provides a model set that any company can adopt as their own. However, if a company wishes to make changes to these, that is possible, as long as the correct procedures are followed.

There are other detailed rules to learn governing the objects (lawful activities), name and registered office of a company.

Chapter overview

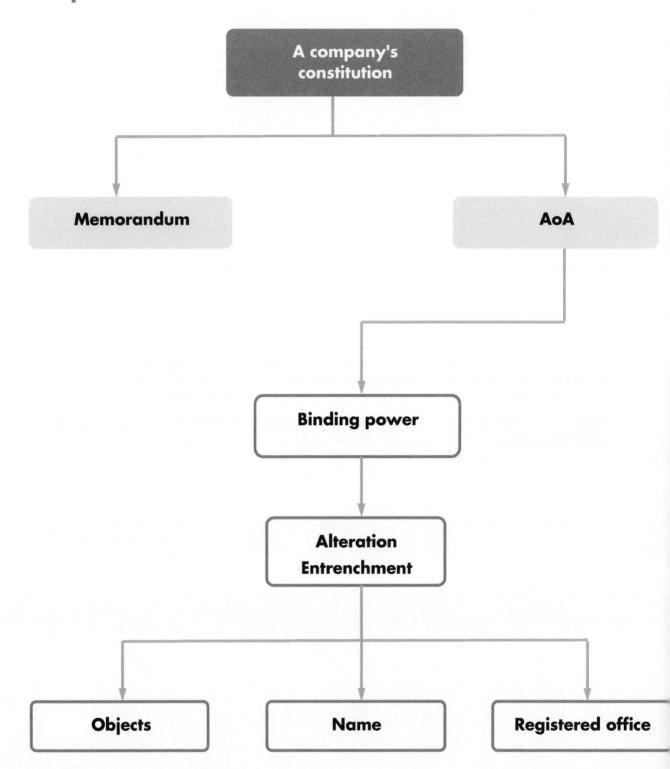

1 Memorandum

Key term

The **Memorandum of Association** (MoA) is a largely historic document that, once submitted to the Registrar, is unalterable.

1.1 It serves to merely record the initial shareholders upon formation of the company.

Activity 1: Memorandum of Association

Required

The Memorandum of Association of a company must be signed by:

A   All the directors and the company secretary
B   One director only
C   The subscribers and the company secretary
D   The subscribers

Solution

2 Articles

Key term

The **Articles of Association** (AoA) are the working part of the constitution that has now absorbed much of the content that used to be the preserve of the MoA.

2.2 The AoA provide the rules by which a company is run and primarily govern the following areas:

(a)   Directors' powers and responsibilities
(b)   Decision making by directors
(c)   Appointment of directors
(d)   Organisation and conduct of general meetings
(e)   Issue and transference of shares
(f)   Payment of dividends
(g)   Exercise of members' rights.

2.3 Additionally when forming a company the promoter will need to consider the rules governing the following:

(a)   Company's **objects** – Section 5
(b)   Company's **name** – Section 6
(c)   Company's **registered office** – Section 7.

BPP
LEARNING MEDIA

3 Binding power of the AoA

3.1 The AoA have the following binding powers.

3.2 **Members to the company**

The company is able to compel the members to obey the AoA – *Hickman v Kent or Romney Marsh Sheep Breeders Association* **(1)**

3.3 **Company to the members**

The members are able to compel the company to obey the AoA – *Pender v Lushington* **(2)**.

3.4 **Members to the members**

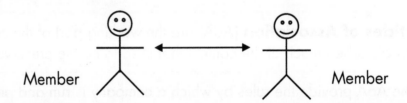

The members are able to compel each other to obey the AoA – *Rayfield v Hands* **(3)**.

3.5 In summary only the following parties are bound by the AoA.

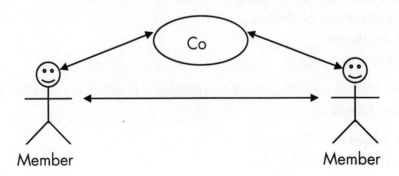

3.6 It was established in the case of *Eley v Positive Life Co* **(4)** that third parties **cannot** enforce the AoA.

Activity 2: Articles of Association

Required

The Articles of Association binds which of the following?

A   The company and its directors
B   The company and its members
C   The directors and members *inter se*
D   The company members only

Solution

---

4   Altering the AoA

4.1 The government has published model AoA for the various types of companies form (private limited by share/guarantee, public) that can be adopted upon incorporation. However, these models can be altered by:

(a)   passing a special resolution

and

(b)   providing the alteration has been made '**bona fide in the interest of the company as a whole**' as per *Greenhalgh v Arderne Cinemas* **(5).**

4.2 The courts are deeply suspicious of any attempt to alter the AoA in any way that allows for the expulsion of a member. Such alterations will only be permitted in the following circumstances:

(a)   Member is defrauding the company
(b)   Member is competing against the company.

Illustration 1

Kirk owns 80% of the shares in Enterprise Ltd, the other shares are held by Scottie. As well as his shareholding in Enterprise Ltd, Scottie is the owner of another company, Vulcan Engineering Ltd (Vulcan). Vulcan historically purchased flux capacitors from Enterprise, but Scottie was dissatisfied with the quality of recent purchases, so switched the custom to a rival firm, Klingon Supplies.

In response to this Kirk passed a special resolution to 'Allow the company by Ordinary Resolution to compulsorily purchase the shares of any member at fair price'. Following this Kirk used his shareholder to pass such a resolution, at which point Scottie refused to sell his shares.

Should this dispute go to court Scottie is bound to win. The alteration by Kirk is too wide, and per case law would fall foul of the 'bona fide' test.

Entrenchment

4.3 It is not possible to declare part or the whole of the AoA unalterable (entrenchment); however, partial entrenchment is possible upon incorporation by notifying the Registrar.

4.4 Conditional entrenchment may require that certain sections of the AoA require a majority in excess of a special resolution in order to be changed/repealed. However, it is not possible to prevent alteration where there is unanimous agreement in favour of change.

5 Objects

5.1 Historically a company was required to state the scope of its lawful activities in a measure designed to protect the interests of shareholders. However, this was eroded by the introduction of the 'general commercial company' clause in the Companies Act 1989 allowing a company to enter into any lawful commercial contract.

5.2 Per the CA 06 all companies will have unrestricted objects, **unless** the AoA are expressly altered to restrict them.

5.3 Any restriction of the objects will be binding on the company and its directors only, meaning that third parties are, usually protected. For example, if the company were to enter into a transaction beyond the scope of its restricted articles, the following could occur;

(a) If the transaction is completed – the company may then take action against the directors for breach of duty in respect of not complying with the company's constitution. The contract with the third party will be valid

or

(b) If the transaction is not completed – the members may seek an injunction, bringing into doubt the validity of the third party contract.

Activity 3: Objects clause

If a transaction falls outside of activities defined by a company's restricted objects clause, what is its status?

A   Valid as against third parties
B   Void as being *ultra vires*
C   Voidable by the third party
D   Voidable by the company

Solution

6 Name

6.1 The **name** of the company must end in the words 'Limited' or 'public limited company' (or abbreviations 'Ltd'/'plc') and be approved by the Registrar, who may refuse to register any name on the following grounds.

   (a)   The name is already in existence

   (b)   Its use would constitute a criminal offence

   (c)   It would be offensive

   (d)   It requires the permission of the Secretary of State (words such as king, royal).

6.2 The full name of the company must be disclosed outside all places of business and on all business documents. Failure to comply with this renders the company secretary personally liable for default and constitutes a criminal offence.

6.3 The name of the company can be changed by **special resolution**. In addition to forwarding a copy of the resolution, the Registrar must separately receive notice of the change of name.

6.4 The company may be forced to change its name by order of the Secretary of State if misleading information has been supplied or if the name adopted is deemed to be too similar to an existing company.

6.5 The **Companies Name Adjudicator** will hear appeals from individuals and companies over similar names. His findings will be published within 90 days and he has the power to order the change of name. In such cases, the adjudicator will presume the name has been legitimately registered. Alternatively, an action may be brought under the common law as per the **tort of passing off**.

7 Registered office

7.1 The **registered office** clause states the country in which the company is domiciled. The domicile can only be changed by an Act of Parliament. As well as being the home of many of the company's statutory books (Section 6) the registered office is where legal notice can be served on the company. The actual address must fall within the **domicile** of the company (England or Wales).

7.2 The registered office address can be changed upon notice to the Registrar. The new address must fall within the company domicile and is only effective upon receipt of notice by the Registrar. The old address remains a valid postal address for 14 days after receipt of notice.

7.3 Certain records must be kept available for inspection at the registered office (as seen in an earlier Chapter).

Chapter summary

- The **Memorandum** is a simple document which states that the subscribers wish to form a company and become members of it.

- A company's constitution comprises the **Articles of Association** and any resolutions and agreements it makes which affect the constitution.

- The articles may be **altered by a special resolution**. The basic test is whether the alteration is for the **benefit of the company as a whole**.

- A company's **objects** are its aims and purposes. If a company enters into a contract which is outside its objects, that contract is said to be **ultra vires**. However, the rights of third parties to the contract are protected.

- The articles constitute a **contract** between:

    - Company and members
    - Members and the company
    - Members and members.

- The articles do not constitute a contract between the company and **third parties**, or members in a capacity other than as members (the **Eley** case).

- The constitution can be used to establish the terms of a **contract existing elsewhere**.

- Shareholders' agreements sometimes supplement a company's constitution.

- Except in certain circumstances, the name must end with the words limited (**Ltd**), public limited company (**plc**) or the Welsh equivalents.

- No company may use a name which is:

    - The **same as an existing company** on the Registrar's index of company names
    - A **criminal offence**, offensive or 'sensitive'
    - Suggest a **connection with the government** or local authority (unless approved).

Activity answers

Activity 1: Memorandum of Association

D   The memorandum is signed by the original subscribers to the company's share capital.

Activity 2: Articles of Association

B   The articles form a binding contract between the company and its members only.

Activity 3: Objects clause

A   *Ultra vires* contracts are valid in respect of third parties. The shareholders can seek an injunction to block such a contract, or, take action against the directors for a breach of their duties.

1 Which of the following persons are not bound to one another by the constitution?

   A   Members to company
   B   Company to members
   C   Members to members
   D   Company to third parties

2 Percy Limited has recently formed a contract with a third party which is restricted by the objects in the company's constitution.

   Which of the following statements is **incorrect**?

   A   The validity of the act cannot be questioned on the grounds of lack of capacity by reason of anything in the company's constitution.

   B   The act may be restrained by the members of Percy Ltd.

   C   The act may be enforced by the company and the third party.

   D   The directors have a duty to observe any limitation on their powers flowing from the company's constitution.

3 A company has been formed within the last six months. Another long-established company considers that because of similarity between names, there may be confusion between it and the new company. The only action the long-established company can take is to bring a passing-off action if it is to prevent the new company using its name

   True   ☐
   False ☐

4 Which of the following would be a valid alteration of a company's articles of association?

   A   An alteration which permits the directors to defraud customers

   B   An alteration which compels members to subscribe for additional shares

   C   An alteration which benefits a small minority of members rather than the company as a whole

   D   An alteration which gives members additional votes if they face removal from the company

5 A company's articles of association will always override the Companies Act 2006?

   True   ☐
   False ☐

Case summaries

1 Hickman v Kent or Romney Marsh Sheep Breeders Association

The articles provided that disputes between members and the association be resolved by arbitration. Hickman brought an action against the company in the courts. It was held that the association were entitled to have the action stayed as the articles constituted a contract between Hickman and the association in respect of their rights as members.

2 Pender v Lushington

AoA stated maximum votes to be attached to shareholdings. P transferred shares to nominee companies in order to increase his votes. The chairman of the company, at a general meeting, disallowed these votes. It was held that this was improper. P could enforce this provision against the company.

3 Rayfield v Hands

The directors of a company were forced to abide by the AoA, which required them to purchase the shares of any members who wished to transfer their shares.

4 Eley v Positive Life Co

E, a solicitor, drafted the original articles and included a provision that the company must always employ him as its solicitor. E became a member of the company some months after its incorporation. He later sued the company for breach of contract in not employing him as a solicitor. It was held that E could not rely on the article, since it was a contract between the company and its members and he was not asserting any claim as a member.

5 Greenhalgh v Arderne Cinemas

An alteration of the AoA to remove pre-emption rights, while depriving G of his individual shareholder rights, was held to be for the benefit of the company as a whole.

Test your learning – answers

Chapter 1

1   False – The law sets the minimum level of acceptable behaviour expected by society from individuals and corporations.

2   A   Corporate Reporting Review Committee
    D   Case Management Committee

    The other bodies are part of the Codes and Standards committee, and are in fact 'councils' not committees.

3   True – The law always takes priority over other rules.

4   A, B, D – Professionalism is not listed amongst the seven principles of public life; all of the others are.

5   B – A framework-based approach sets out general principles of behaviour and general guidelines, giving advice on how to handle certain circumstances.

Chapter 2

1   C – Scepticism and independence are professional qualities expected of an accountant, but not fundamental principles.

2   (i)   Reliability
    (ii)   Responsibility
    (iii)   Timeliness
    (iv)   Courtesy
    (v)   Respect

3   B – Act follows Design in CIMA's professional development cycle.

4   A – Integrity describes the principle of straightforwardness and honesty and not being party to the supply of false information. Option B describes objectivity, C relates to professional competence and D relates to confidentiality.

5   C – Objectivity requires an accountant to avoid bias, conflicts of interest or the influence of others in their work.

Chapter 3

1   True – This is a description of corporate values.

2   C – Whilst Jack has no moral objections to the policy, he has been required to act in an illegal way by his employer. There is therefore tension between societal values (the law) and corporate values (the employment policy).

3   False – It is contractual obligations which are voluntary to fulfil.

4   B – Objectivity is a professional value.

5   True – CIMA has such an ethical helpline.

Chapter 4

1   Directed, controlled

2   A – Lack of board involvement

      D – Inadequate supervision

3   False – The UK has taken a principles-based approach, as seen in its Corporate Governance Code, whereas the American approach is to use rules, embodied in the Sarbanes-Oxley legislation.

4   B – The main cause cited is the agency problem as a result of the separation of ownership and the control of companies.

5   D – The OECD Principles of Corporate Governance form the international benchmark

Chapter 5

1   D – The UK Corporate Governance Code recommends that non-executives have enough of a presence to prevent domination of the board by small groups or individuals.

2   B – The UK Corporate Governance Code states that the chief executive should not go on to be chairman at a later date.

3   False – They are generally staffed by non-executive directors.

4   C – Compliance – the five main sections of the UK code are Leadership, Effectiveness, Accountability, Remuneration and Relations with shareholders.

5   D – The UK code operates on a principles basis that requires compliance or explanation for non-compliance.

Chapter 6

1   A, B, D will all help to prevent fraud. References help root out dishonest candidates, Codes of Ethics reinforce a strong culture, and Segregation of Duty adds supervision. Whistleblowing will help detect, rather than prevent fraud.

2   C – The small company exemption looks at staff numbers (<50), turnover (<10.2m) and net assets (<5.1m) and a company must meet at least two of these criteria.

3   True – Whilst this statement is correct, if the external auditor becomes aware of a fact, that, had it been known at the date of the auditor's report, may have caused him to change his opinion, then should raise this with the client and discuss with management whether the financial statements need amending.

4   C – The internal auditors should report to both management and the audit committee to ensure their work is free from bias eg failing to adequately criticise management. It is the external auditors who report to shareholders.

5   False – Companies are free to justify not having an internal audit function; if they wish to have one, they can provide this internally or can outsource.

Chapter 7

1   A – One of the main potential benefits of integrated reporting is that it helps organisations identify more clearly the links between financial and non-financial performance. Integrated reporting focuses on value generation in a broad sense, not only in a narrow financial sense (eg in terms of revenue or profit). Therefore option (iii) is not true.

Option (i) reflects the guiding principle that an integrated report should provide an insight into an organisation's strategic focus and future orientation.

Option (ii) reflects the guiding principle that an integrated report should provide an insight into an organisation's relationships with its key stakeholders.

2   A and C – These are part of the seven principles. B refers to the fair presentation of financial statements, and D is close to Stakeholder Relationships, but is not the same.

3   False – CSR is a very wide area that looks at the whole interaction of a company with its environment. By contrast, ethics is a narrower field that sits within CSR.

4   A Integrated – Beta's approach sees its brand and CSR operate in synchrony.

5   False – Whilst good CSR policies may increase the value of an organisation's brand, there are other factors at play eg the perceived quality of goods and services delivered.

Chapter 8

1   Offer and acceptance, consideration, intention to create legal relations.

2   True – A conveyance must be evidenced by deed.

3   D – Requesting information does not terminate an offer.

A is termination by lapse of time – B is revocation by the offeror – C is an offer is terminated when it is accepted.

4   (1) communicated (2) offeror (3) offer (4) information (5) invitation to treat (6) rejection

5   True

6   D – An offer cannot also be acceptance.

Chapter 9

1 True – As a rule, past consideration is not 'good', though there is an exception if it can be proven there was an earlier implied promise to pay.

2 (1) adequate (2) sufficient

3 D – False. Social, domestic and family arrangements are not generally intended to be binding. Commercial agreements are generally intended to be binding.

4 (1) commercial (2) domestic

5 The correct answers are: Payment in kind and Payment by a third person.

    The others are incorrect – payment must be earlier, not deferred. Collateral contracts are an exception to the privity rule. Payment must be at a new, not agreed location. Payment can be via any type of consideration – executed or executory.

Chapter 10

1 True – Silence can only be a misrepresentation in unusual circumstances such as applying for insurance, or when earlier statements are no longer true.

2 B – A misrepresentation is:

    (i) A statement of fact which proves to be untrue

    (ii) Made by one party to the other before the contract is formed in order to induce the latter to enter into the contract

    (iii) A statement which affects the claimant's judgement.

3 False – damages for fraudulent misrepresentation are claimed under the tort of deceit. The MRA 1967 awards damages for negligent misrepresentation.

4 Beyonce has perpetrated a fraudulent misrepresentation against Kelly – <u>False</u>, Beyonce had an honestly held belief that the vase was authentic.

    Michelle may have committed an innocent misrepresentation against Beyonce – <u>True</u>, Michelle may have been duped herself if she bought the vase with the certificate of authentication.

    Kelly could rescind the contract and return the vase to Kelly – <u>False</u>, if Kelly wishes to rescind the contract, this must be done against the person who sold it to her, Beyonce.

    Beyonce may have perpetrated a negligent misrep against Kelly – <u>True</u>, it is possible that Beyonce could have taken steps herself to authenticate the vase before re-selling it eg taking it to an independent valuer.

5 (1) fact (2) before (3) untrue [or false] (4) induce

Chapter 11

1   B – A term may be implied into a contract by

-    Statute

-    Trade practice unless an express term overrides it

-    The court giving effect to a term which the parties had agreed upon but failed to express because it was obvious.

2   (1) condition (2) discharged (3) damages (4) warranty (5) subsidiary (6) breach

3   C – Wario's failure to train would likely constitute a breach of warranty (see *Bettini v Gye*), but his failure to turn up to play is much more serious and is likely to be a breach of condition (see *Poussard v Spiers*) and therefore would give the club the right to rescind his contract, and sue him for damages.

4   B - The parties are entitled to leave an essential term to be settled by other means, for example setting the price by reference to open market value, arbitration or a previous course of dealing.

5   EVT Ltd can recover damages from DTZ Ltd and avoid the contract.   False
     EVT may only recover damages   True
     EVT can consider the contract as repudiated   False
     EVT may consider the contract as repudiated or recover damages.   False

     The only true remedy available for breach of warranty is to recover damages.

Chapter 12

1   True – Businesses are classed as consumers if they can prove the contract was not made in the ordinary course of their business.

2   (a) and (2)

     (b) and (1)

3   B – The 'main purpose' rule states that a court should assume that an exclusion clause is not intended to defeat the main purpose of the contact.

4   C – Exclusion clauses cannot limit liability for personal injury or death. Onerous obligations must be sufficiently highlighted or they will be treated as not incorporated in the contract. However, they do have a legitimate use in business by allocating risk between organisations.

5   Incorporated   *Contra proferentum*

Chapter 13

1   (1)   Control test

    (2)   Integration test

    (3)   Multiple (economic reality) test

2   False – All employees are entitled to an itemised payslip from the day they start working.

3   D – All these options are available, although care must be taken to avoid constructive or unfair dismissal cases.

4   B – Employers do not have a duty to provide a reference.

5   The employer is vicariously liable for the employee's torts **in the course of his employment**

    Employers are **liable** if an employee commits a tort whilst disobeying instructions during the course of their work.

    Employers are **not liable** for torts committed in a company vehicle when the employee is undertaking private business.

    Employers are **liable** when an employee defrauds a client to his own advantage in the course of his employment.

Chapter 14

1   True – Employees whose roles have been outsourced are protected by the Transfer of Undertaking rules.

2   True – This is the framework for health and safety in the UK.

3   False – The Bribery Act applies to private and public employees worldwide.

4   C – This is correct. In respect of option A, this is at the discretion of the court. With respect to B and D the Act affords protection to the worker rather than imposing sanctions on the employer.

5   C – Dealing is an offence connected to insider dealing, the others are the offences associated with money laundering.

6   Lawful processing + Accurate + Transfer outside Europe are amongst the eight principles of data processing. The other options are part of the rights afforded to data subjects.

Chapter 15

1   B – 2/12 × £24,000. He was already given 1/12 (one month's notice) by Chingtow.

2   B – Wrongful dismissal is a common law action and damages are the only remedy.

3   True – Unfair treatment of a woman by reason of her pregnancy is sex discrimination.

4   (1) compensation (2) qualifying (3) dismissed (4) employer (5) reason (6) employment tribunal (7) three

5   D – Enforcing rights to a maximum working week – all of the others are potentially fair reasons.

Chapter 16

1   B – A written agreement is not needed.

2   B – Members only have a liability for any outstanding amounts of share capital partly paid for.

3   True – Corporate personality is the principle that companies are legally distinct from their owners.

4   D – In a partnership, the partners extract drawings on which they pay income tax. Partnerships do not themselves pay tax, partners are not employees and are therefore not taxed through the PAYE system, nor do they receive dividends from the partnership.

5   False – Sole trader businesses are not legally distinct from their owners.

Chapter 17

1   A and D are correct – A private company cannot sell its shares to the public on any stock market, so B is incorrect. Directors need not have unlimited liability, so C is incorrect.

2   C – The directors are punished for allowing the company to trade before it is allowed to.

3   False – The company must make a new contract on similar terms.

4   True – A distinguishing feature of a public company is the need to appoint a Company Secretary, this post is optional for more private companies.

5   B – As long as the company is registered before the date that the contract (which the promoter wants it to be a party to) is signed, then the company can ratify that contract.

Chapter 18

1   A, B and C are correct. D is incorrect, illustrated by *Eley v Positive Life Co*

2   B – A, C and D are true. Members can only act before the contract is signed, so B is incorrect.

3   False – The long-established company can also complain to the Company Names Adjudicator.

4   D – Such an alteration would be valid. Alterations may not contravene general law (as in A), compel members to subscribe for additional shares (B) or not be *bona fide* in the interests of the company as a whole.

5   False – The Companies Act 2006 will override a company's articles where it prohibits a company doing something.

Bibliography

Charities Aid Foundation UK Giving 2015 (May 2016), Retrieved from: www.cafonline.org:

https://www.cafonline.org/docs/default-source/personal-giving/caf_ukgiving2015_1891a_web_230516.pdf?sfvrsn=2

CIMA Ethics checklist. Retrieved from www.cimaglobal.com:

http://www.cimaglobal.com/Professional-ethics/Ethics/Responsible-business/Ethics-checklist/

OECD. (2015). G20/OECD Principles of Corporate Governance, Retrieved from: www.oecd.org

http://dx.doi.org/10.1787/9789264236882-en

IFAC (2012), Integrating Governance for Sustainable Success, Retrieved from: www.ifac.org

https://www.ifac.org/publications-resources/integrating-governance-sustainable-success

CIMA Simple, practical proposals for better reporting of corporate governance. Retrieved from www.cimaglobal.com:

http://www.cimaglobal.com/Documents/Thought_leadership_docs/Governance/Report-Leadership-Corporate-Governance-Report.pdf

Financial Reporting Council (April 2016), The UK Corporate Governance Code Retrieved from: www.frc.org.uk

https://www.frc.org.uk/Our-Work/Publications/Corporate-Governance/UK-Corporate-Governance-Code-April-2016.pdf

Sweney, M. (2016) 'James Murdoch's return as Sky chair is a major concern, says investor', The Guardian, 29 January Retrieved from: www.theguardian.com/

https://www.theguardian.com/global/2016/jan/29/james-murdochs-return-as-sky-chair-is-a-major-concern-says-investor

Marks and Spencer (2016), Plan A Report 2015, Retrieved from: www.marksandspencer.com

http://corporate.marksandspencer.com/media/6e633a181b124309bab60137c8171017

Fisk, M, Calkins, L (2011) 'BP's Pursuit of Cost-Cutting Led to Gulf Spill, Lawyers Say', Bloomberg, 5 February, Retrieved from: www.bloomberg.com/

http://www.bloomberg.com/news/articles/2011-02-05/bp-mismanagement-led-to-explosion-spill-lawsuit-says-update1-

Eversheds Sweett Group sentenced after first ever corporate conviction for failing to prevent bribery, Retrieved from: www.eversheds.com

http://www.eversheds.com/global/en/what/articles/index.page?ArticleID=en/Fraud_and_financial_crime/Sweett_group_sentenced

Index

REVIEW FORM

How have you used this Course Book?
(Tick one box only)

☐ Self study

☐ On a course_____

☐ Other _____

Why did you decide to purchase this Course Book? *(Tick one box only)*

☐ Have used BPP materials in the past

☐ Recommendation by friend/colleague

☐ Recommendation by a college lecturer

☐ Saw advertising

☐ Other _____

During the past six months do you recall seeing/receiving either of the following?
(Tick as many boxes as are relevant)

☐ Our advertisement in Financial Management

☐ Our Publishing Catalogue

Which (if any) aspects of our advertising do you think are useful?
(Tick as many boxes as are relevant)

☐ Prices and publication dates of new editions

☐ Information on Course Book content

☐ Details of our free online offering

☐ None of the above

Your ratings, comments and suggestions would be appreciated on the following areas of this Course Book.

	Very useful	Useful	Not useful
Chapter overviews	☐	☐	☐
Introductory section	☐	☐	☐
Quality of explanations	☐	☐	☐
Illustrations	☐	☐	☐
Chapter activities	☐	☐	☐
Test your learning	☐	☐	☐
Keywords	☐	☐	☐

	Excellent	Good	Adequate	Poor
Overall opinion of this Course Book	☐	☐	☐	☐

Do you intend to continue using BPP Products? ☐ Yes ☐ No

Please note any further comments and suggestions/errors on the reverse of this page and return it to:
BPP Publishing Services, Aldine Place, 142-144 Uxbridge Road, London, W12 8AA

The BPP author of this edition can be e-mailed at: lmfeedback@bpp.com

REVIEW FORM (continued)

TELL US WHAT YOU THINK

Please note any further comments and suggestions/errors below